POWER TOOLS
F O R   M E N

A Blueprint for Healthy Masculinity

Leonard Szymczak
& Rick Broniec

GPS BOOKS

Praise for *Power Tools for Men*

"This is a down-to-earth breakthrough book that weaves heart-felt stories with practical concepts that promote healthy masculinity and help men thrive in the 21st century."

— Jack Canfield, *New York Times* bestselling co-creator
of the *Chicken Soup for the Soul*® series

"If I had a nickel for every time a woman sighed in despair wondering where the conscious men were, I'd be a wealthy woman. Thank God I now have an answer. They are reading Power Tools for Men! Szymczak and Broniec have cracked the code on modern masculinity. No more modeling manhood after our distant, dominating fathers! The new man is an awakened, mature, and integrated man who is connected to the power of his heart. Women, buy this book for the men you love, and men, buy this book to finally know how to step into your true power and destiny."

—Katherine Woodward Thomas, *New York Times* bestselling author
of *Conscious Uncoupling: 5 Steps to Living Happily Ever After* and
Calling in "The One": 7 Weeks to Attract the Love of Your Life

"Rick Broniec and Leonard Szymczak answer the question, 'What the hell is happening to men?' Their book provides a powerful roadmap for men during these turbulent times. By sharing their personal stories and those of men who have been touched by their work over the past thirty years, they empower men to open their hearts and embrace healthy masculinity. This book is a must for men and the women who love them or are raising sons."

—Rich Tosi, Founding President, ManKind Project

"*Power Tools for Men* is a crucial and foundational message for the evolution of consciousness. As the mother of a son who has grown up in this confusing time, I feel the unresolved pain of masculinity that has not found its gorgeous new expression into our world. As a teacher dedicated to shared awakening of unity and evolutionary love, I celebrate Leonard and Rick's brilliance in bringing forth exactly what is needed to support men in finding their place in the new future we are being pulled towards."

—Patricia Albere, Evolutionary Collective Founder
and bestselling author of *Evolutionary Relationships:
Unleashing the Power of Mutual Awakening*

"I love this book! It touched me to tears as I read the healing stories… men's real stories… including the authors surviving their own crises. This is real deal men's work… dive in… you are not alone!"

—Bill Kauth, Co-founder of the ManKind Project,
author of *A Circle of Men* and with Zoe Alowan, *We
Need Each Other: Building Gift Community*

"Leonard and Rick offer men a simple, yet effective, guide for navigating the confusing challenges we face in the 21st century. They bring years of experience and the power of two leaders who have been doing men's work for many years. In these confusing times, it's refreshing to read a book that cuts through the maze of conflicting views to bring men together. Unlike many books that heighten the conflict between men and women, *Power Tools for Men* offers men and women the opportunity to come together to end the battle of the sexes. As someone who has been involved in men's work for fifty years now, I consider Leonard and Rick colleagues in our joint efforts to bring about a world that is worth passing on to our children, grandchildren, and future generations."

—Jed Diamond, PhD, author of *12 Rules for Good Men*
and *The Irritable Male Syndrome: Understanding and
Managing the 4 Key Causes of Depression and Aggression*

"This book was a real eye-opener for me. Not only did it help me better understand my husband and son, but as an attorney mediator for the past 33 years, it helped me gain insight into the issues that men face. Through Rick and Leonard's own stories and experiences working with men, readers will gain keen insight into the challenges facing the male psyche in our society. In the era of #MeToo, this book is a must read for men and women!"

—Mari Frank, attorney, radio host, and co-author of
Fighting for Love: Turn Conflict into Intimacy

Other Books by Leonard Szymczak

The Roadmap Home: Your GPS to Inner Peace

Bob Cratchit's Christmas Carol

Tiny Tim's Christmas Carol

Kookaburra's Last Laugh

Cuckoo Forevermore

Fighting for Love: Turn Conflict into Intimacy
Coauthored with Mari Frank

Other Books by Rick Broniec

A Passionate Life: 7 Steps for Reclaiming Your Passion, Purpose and Joy

The Seven Generations Story: An Incentive to Heal Yourself, Your Family and the Planet

Disclaimer: This publication is meant to provide information about men's healing and personal growth. It is not meant to replace therapy. Everyone has unique concerns and should seek professional advice when appropriate. Clients who are mentioned in this book have had their names and aspects of their identity altered to protect confidentiality.

Library of Congress Control Number: 2023904586

Authors: Szymczak, Leonard and Broniec, Rick

Title: *Power Tools for Men: A Blueprint for Healthy Masculinity*

Published by GPS Books, Dana Point, California, 92629

ISBN – 979-8-9869027-3-9 (ebook)
ISBN – 979-8-9869027-4-6 (paperback)

Cover Design: Fiona Jayde
Interior Design: Tamara Cribley
Editors: Mary Harris & Glenda Rynn
Author Photos: Esperanza H.S. Photography Department

Printed in the United States of America
1. Self-help/Men. 2. Personal Growth. 3. Masculinity. 4. Gender Studies

"Begin each day with the blueprint of my deepest values FIRMLY in mind, then when challenges come, make decisions BASED on those values."

— Stephen R. Covey

"The future of men is a new and elevated stature gained through personal growth, greater balance of work and personal lives, positive role models, and newly defined perceptions of masculinity."

— Jack Myers

"Champions come and go, but to be legendary you got to have heart, more heart than the next man, more than anyone in the world."

— Muhammad Ali

Table of Contents

Foreword

In October of 2017, I stood on the carpet at the Mankind Project Warrior Weekend and spoke my truth. I was surrounded by men, some facilitators, and some, like me, who were first-time attendees. I said, "I don't like men. I don't trust men. I hate men." It seemed a weak and shameful admission. And then, after a long pause I said, "And I'm sick to death of being alone." And there it was, the most shameful admission of all. I was 57 years old.

The story of men is a story of deep disconnection and loneliness. Cigna Health released a study in 2020 revealing that more than half of US adults surveyed report sometimes or always feeling alone (52%). That's over 125 million people struggling with loneliness. The bullying, hyper-competitive ways boys and men are taught about masculinity play a huge role in this epidemic of isolation. Chronic loneliness has a health impact equal to smoking a pack of cigarettes a day, leading to dramatically higher levels of heart disease, neurodegenerative diseases, diabetes, cancer, depression, and more.

In Professor Niobe Way's book *Deep Secrets*, her research reveals how, by late adolescence, boys disengage from their close boyhood friendships. These same boys in early adolescence said they "loved" their best friends and that "they would go crazy without them." Way's research on masculine culture reveals that boys are under constant pressure to express not who they authentically are, but instead to prove what they are not, specifically "little kids, girly, or gay." In their rush to align with our culture of masculinity's narrow limiting view of manhood, boys give up their close male friendships, at which point their suicide rates become four times that of girls their age, their loneliness and loss looming large in that single brutal statistic.

And so, cut off from connection, we are left to align with a dominance-based culture of masculinity, which is all about what we do, not who we authentically are. Competing for status in dominance culture fuels constant anxiety for men. It is anxiety born out of a singular kind of fear: that we are not enough. That we're not making enough money, not having enough sex, not winning enough, not dominating enough, not outperforming other men enough to prove we are "real men." Dominance-based masculinity doesn't care who we authentically are.

I wrote a number of years ago and I continue to believe it's true: "We're wasting our lives chasing a fake rabbit around a track, all the while convinced there's meat to be had. There is no meat. We are the meat." It doesn't matter what we did yesterday, did we do it again today?

Men have been sold a bill of goods that trains us out of authentic, meaningful connection and into relentless bullying competition. This all happens before we are even old enough to understand what is lost to us. The result for men, and for those whose lives we impact, is broken relationships, depression, isolation, addiction, violence, and early mortality.

I tried to live up to the rules of our culture of dominance-based masculinity for more than fifty years. After two divorces, innumerable professional failures, a lifetime of disconnection, drinking, drugs, and anger, I knew I was looking down a dark road with a very bad ending. A friend said, "Try the ManKind Project Warrior Weekend." After refusing for months, I finally relented and went. And so began "doing my work" in partnership with a community of men who most certainly do care about who I authentically am. These men invited me into connection, friendship, self-reflection, and community.

The Mankind Project is only one of the many ways men can begin doing their work. We can seek out a therapist who understands men's work. We can seek out healthy masculinity podcasts or videos. Or we can read books like the one you are holding in your hands.

The authors of *Power Tools for Men: A Blueprint for Healthy Masculinity*, Rick Broniec and Leonard Szymczak, represent decades of shared experience in facilitating healthy masculinity work. Their reputation as honest, wise, curious leaders in our field is unimpeachable. Their book is a pathway into men's work informed by two powerful points of entry. Rick is an MKP Warrior Weekend leader. Leonard is a psychotherapist who specializes in working with men and couples. Between them, they have seventy years' experience in facilitating healthy masculinity work.

The ways Leonard and Rick break down the issues men face will give readers a deep and layered understanding of how our culture of masculinity has blocked our potential for connection, our ability to be in community, and our capacity to love ourselves and others. As you read their book, listen for the acceptance and compassion in which this work is rooted.

A particular kind of compassion is demonstrated in the ways these two men share their own stories of disconnection, confirming that all of us have those stories. They unravel the intersection between their own personal struggles and the larger cultural influences that harm us all. In this way, they offer the gold that men in the work once passed on to them: self-compassion and self-acceptance. It is at the heart of Rick and Leonard's book and at the core of men's work, the universal invitation to release our shame and accept our whole selves. It is personal work that never ends, but as Rick and Leonard so eloquently share, in healthy masculinity work we walk a path of friendship, connection, and self-discovery. We get powerful opportunities to support others. We come to know and understand our better selves. Those in our lives come to trust us and love us more deeply.

Power Tools for Men: A Blueprint for Healthy Masculinity offers the CLASSICS Model as a pathway to connection, a way in out of the dark and cold of isolation. If you know a man who is struggling, this book represents a path to something so much better—a community of connection, support, growth, and compassion.

Men are waiting to welcome us in this work. We need only reach out and ask for help.

Mark Greene, author of *The Little #MeToo Book for Men* and co-host of *Remaking Manhood: The Healthy Masculinity* Podcast

New York City, 2023

Preface

Men cannot change if there are no blueprints for change.

— bell hooks

Men are in Crisis. With mass shootings across America occurring at a rate of more than two per day[1], it's no wonder that the phrase *toxic masculinity* has entered our vocabulary. The question needs to be answered, "Is masculinity inherently toxic?" Our answer is a resounding NO. We believe that men are inherently good, decent, noble, and responsible. However, we can't deny that some of our behaviors are toxic. Therefore, we need to address the question: What can we do about behaviors that hurt ourselves, others, and relationships?

Consider these horrifying statistics: Men commit almost 98% of mass shootings; perpetrate 90% of homicides in America, are victims of homicide 78% of the time, make up 93% percent of the prison population, and commit suicide seven times more often than women. Seventy percent of substance abuse treatment admissions are male with the alcohol abuse rate for men being twice that of women. In addition, the #MeToo movement has highlighted male sexual harassment by Hollywood, corporate, and political figures. Furthermore, the Men's Rights Activists (MRA) and the

---

1   www.massshootingtracker.site

Involuntary Celibacy (Incel) movement promote open hatred and violence toward women.

These statistics clearly show that some of men's behaviors, not masculinity itself, are toxic and destructive to themselves and others. The purpose of this book is to help men transform from toxic to healthy masculinity.

In August 2018 the American Psychological Association, citing more than forty years of experience, issued its first-ever set of guidelines about boys and men, stating that "traditional masculine ideology" harms men's mental health. Traditional masculinity includes an emphasis on physical strength, achievement, competitiveness, self-reliance, toughness, aggression, avoidance of weakness, stoicism, restricted emotional expression, sexual prowess, dominance, and the avoidance of anything deemed feminine.

There are many reasons for these traditional traits. Some have been developed over time when men were hunters and had to provide food for their family. Aggression, power, self-reliance, and physical endurance were vital to fulfill that role. However, those qualities prevented men from acknowledging vulnerability and seeking help when encountering problems.

Becoming a man entailed learning not only what endeavors are consistent with being masculine, but what are considered feminine activities. Since boys have to change their gender identity to be different from the one who has birthed them, they begin to develop an acute sensitivity and ability to discriminate between masculine and feminine behaviors, typically avoiding qualities associated with femininity such as vulnerability, nurturance, sensitivity, gentleness, humility, affection, tenderness, dependence, and emotional intimacy. As a result, men have learned to selectively incorporate behaviors that are considered more manly, and those include being tough, unemotional, aggressive, and even violent.

Being closed off emotionally can lead to loneliness, isolation, and depression. This, coupled with men's tendency to externalize problems and blame others, can translate into rage and violence. The epidemic of mass shootings in the United States is evidence of this. In 2021 there were 818 mass shootings and in 2022 there were 753 mass shootings in the US alone.[2] The devastating toll for these acts of male violence impacts relationships, families, and communities.

In recent years, women's voices have increased in volume and number, thereby inciting a shift of traditional gender roles in commerce, education, politics, relationships, and the household. How do men grapple with the many confusing, contradictory messages? We must be strong, yet also tender and emotional. We must be competitive, yet cooperative. We must initiate, but not be overbearing. We must be protective, but not over-controlling. We must be breadwinners, but also caretakers of children.

These mixed messages create confusion, especially when there's not a clear blueprint for healthier behaviors. If we cling to an outmoded model of masculinity by persisting in stereotypical roles, values, and behaviors, we promote power, hierarchy, aggression, entitlement, and winning at all costs. Some of these behaviors have been described in the media as "toxic masculinity." Again, we don't believe that masculinity is toxic. Rather, some traditional male behaviors are toxic to men, women, and children. It's time to evolve our masculine identity to expand choices for men to be more fully human. However, even if we try to change, most of us will flounder without a blueprint.

Power Tools for Men provides such a blueprint to help men grow up as healthy adults and show up as leaders to serve the world.

HEROES

Great leaders from the past are often portrayed as "classical" heroes. They emulated values and characteristics of noble men in service to

---

2   Ibid.

a just cause. Men like Achilles, Spartacus, Socrates, Plato, and King Arthur and the Knights of the Round Table provided models of loyalty, honor, truth, courage, and wisdom. Men aspired to include these positive qualities in their lives. They withstood hardship to protect others, thought logically to solve problems, maintained a sense of loyalty and commitment, and took courageous risks.

These qualities have served men for thousands of years. Unfortunately, many of them have been perverted over time to become self-serving and self-defeating, creating a traditional model of masculinity that no longer fits for the 21st century. For example, we withstood hardship but, in doing so, created walls of isolation from women and other men. We thought logically but ended up shutting down feelings. Loyalty became blind obedience, and taking risks morphed into reckless aggression, even violence. The result: masculinity in crisis. Men are suffering silently in growing numbers from depression, anxiety, relationship problems, addictions, health-related illnesses, and suicidal and violent behaviors.

We reclaim the word *classics* to highlight a new paradigm of manhood that asks men to become heroes. The acronym *CLASSICS* identifies eight dimensions that promote healthy masculinity:

C = Connection
L = Love
A = Authenticity
S = Spirituality
S = Sexuality
I = Intention
C = Community
S = Sovereignty

These principles lay the foundation for men to rewire their masculine selves, shifting from traditional masculine ideology to the new CLASSICS blueprint, as shown in the comparison below.

Traditional Masculinity (Old Blueprint)	CLASSICS Model (New Blueprint)
Shutting down emotions and disconnecting from relationships	**Connection:** valuing emotions and relationships
Avoiding real intimacy	**Love:** sharing with an open heart
Encouraging toughness and invulnerability	**Authenticity:** relating vulnerably with accountability and integrity
Being performance-driven and materialistic	**Spirituality:** connecting within and with others
Using sex as an act of domination	**Sexuality:** accessing pleasure responsibly
Living in self-serving ways	**Intention:** creating a mission of service
Overvaluing self-reliance and self-sufficiency	**Community:** building a circle of men
Embracing power over others and winning at all costs	**Sovereignty:** leading with your inner King

In the 21st century, men must access a wider range of traits and behaviors, as outlined in the table above, to develop greater resiliency and deal with the maelstrom of change we face today. The eight dimensions increase self-awareness, emotional intelligence, loving relationships, resiliency, spiritual connection, and personal responsibility.

Join us as we share our CLASSICS Model and discover a blueprint that promotes healthy masculinity.

Introduction

We, Leonard and Rick, have been actively involved in the trenches of men's personal growth, each of us with well over thirty-five years of work specializing in men's self-development. We have facilitated workshops in eleven countries on four continents. Together, we've explored issues of masculinity with thousands of men. What we've discovered is confusion, frustration, anger, and grief, along with relief and even excitement about the changing roles of men. What once worked for our forefathers no longer works for us men in the 21st century.

From time immemorial, men have shared stories of challenges, defeats, and conquests. It seems fitting that we share our stories, knowing that they may mirror some of your stories.

⊙ LEONARD'S STORY

In 1984 in Sydney, Australia, I asked myself, "What the hell am I doing with a group of sixty-five strangers—all men?" I had attended a gathering of men who were meeting for the first time in a community center to form support groups. When I looked around the conference room, I felt terror. Could I feel safe with so many men?

Safety was something I grappled with as a child. Growing up in a working-class neighborhood on the South Side of Chicago, I had been terrified of the fights between my parents. On one occasion, my father chased my mother with a knife in front of me and my siblings. When he was admitted to a psychiatric hospital, I was six years old. One and a half years later, he returned from his hospitalization. The family, once again, became a fearful place. I couldn't feel safe around my father, wondering if he would "go crazy" again. When the conflict with my mother continued to escalate, he left for good. I was nine at the time and, though I felt sad, I was relieved that the fighting would subside.

However, my mother was angry and bitter about being abandoned and having to support four children on her own. She worked at the Campbell Soup factory, and with two boys and two girls to feed, her hands were full. Too full to clean, cook, work, and tend children. Too full to cradle a frightened child or whisper, "I love you" to my broken heart. When overwhelmed, she would lash out at my absent father, stating, "All you men are rotten."

To survive my childhood, I shut down and managed my fear, grief, anger, and shame by adopting defenses—silence, avoidance, and suppression, along with a dash of sarcasm and dark humor. I had learned to survive by following the ways of men by being independent and self-sufficient and not expressing my feelings.

However, my underlying anxiety and fear turned into a faint hum coursing through my veins like electricity, urging me to be alert, ever ready, on edge. I ignored the hum and got busy, like other men whom I saw doing exactly that.

It wasn't until after I became a psychotherapist that I realized the damage caused by neglect, abuse, and abandonment. Deeper insidious wounds resulted from the ways I had adapted and accommodated as a man. No talking, no feeling, no crying, no sign of a whimper—even when my heart was humming with pain. Denial and disconnection were not the best ways to manage wounds, yet without much guidance or direction, it was hard to act otherwise.

I longed for a father who not only encouraged and supported me, but also blessed my place in the world as a male. That longing eventually brought me to a men's gathering in 1984. That group in Sydney not only accelerated my healing but challenged me to break the chains of some masculine roles traditionally defined by society—to be competitive, in control, status conscious, invulnerable, unemotional, and achievement driven. Back then, the group evolved into a band of brothers committed to accept, support, encourage, and challenge one another to redefine masculinity.

Since 1984 I've been participating with other men to forge a new model of manhood. I have attended men's weekends, including the New Warrior Training Adventure and the Victories of the Heart and have taught courses on masculinity, male friendship, and therapy with men. My participation in men's personal growth groups in Sydney, Chicago, and now Southern California, has spanned over thirty-five years. These groups have supported me through my divorce after twenty-six years of marriage and sustained me through changes in location, relationships, and life crises. I feel ever so grateful to belong to a band of brothers who embolden me to speak my truth and evolve my masculine self.

I have come to realize that breaking free from the old model isn't easy. It requires courage and dedication to face my wounds, acknowledge my gifts, express my emotions, and share my stories. It also asks me to honor other men and women dedicated to being their authentic selves.

Part of my healing was to work in partnership. I first met Rick at a men's group in Oceanside, California in 2016. From our first encounter, I felt an instant connection. We both hailed from the Midwest and knew many of the leaders of the men's movement. We were committed to personal work and loved to write. Since we both enjoyed each other's company, it was only a matter of time before our writing bromance took off.

I feel truly honored to collaborate with Rick who is a Harley spiritual biker with integrity, compassion, wisdom, and wit. I've hopped on board with Rick to touch your hearts, minds, and souls. One thing's for sure, we're in for a hell of a ride!

RICK'S STORY

What was this kid from Chicago supposed to do to lead a good, happy, and prosperous life? I did what I was told by the men in my life. I worked hard doing three jobs, volunteered to help the needy, attended church regularly, and became a good family man. But those activities didn't bring happiness; instead, they brought me to the verge of collapse, heading toward divorce, with few friends, no one I trusted, and feeling pissed off at God and most members of my family. Back then, confused, lost, and alone, I asked myself, "How did this happen?"

As the oldest child of six siblings, I was seven years old when my parents separated for the first of seven times. That event became seared into my memory. My father had put me on his knee and told me that he wouldn't be living with us. He encouraged me to be strong, take care of my mother, my brothers and sisters, and be the man of the family.

Though he was attempting to show his love and support me in the best way he could, his words became a curse for many years of my life. Being told to be the man of the family pierced my heart and soul. From the age of seven, I lost my childhood—the innocence of being playful and alive—and instantly became an adult. I became my mother's surrogate husband and protector and my siblings' second father. I became super responsible and focused on achievement so that I could look good to the world. At the same time, I became unwilling to admit any faults or acknowledge my needs. I stuffed my emotions and became what author, John Bradshaw, calls a "Human Doing" instead of a "Human Being." In other words, I became a typical American man, believing this was the correct way to be.

Fast forward to 1988. By all outward appearances, I had it made. I was successful and living a wonderful, productive life as a husband, father, teacher, and minister. On the inside, however, a different story unfolded. I felt unfulfilled, frustrated, fragile, and hollow. I didn't know how to express my feelings in productive ways, and I did not feel alive. My marriage and love life were in shambles. I felt like an imposter

4

who didn't deserve all the good I was experiencing. I smiled on the outside and gave the appearance of being well-adjusted and happy. Inside, I was filled with angst, resentment, self-doubt, and fear. Even my daily meditation or the times I led services at my church each week had little meaning. I became a miserable workaholic who lived behind a carefully crafted mask of perfection and invincibility. I taught, parented, and ministered out of a sense of duty, rather than from a well of passion.

Somehow, I knew something had to change. My then-wife and I joined a thirteen-week program of learning about being an adult child of a dysfunctional family. That process and the ongoing support group acted as a major turning point. I learned about family systems and the roles that I, and my siblings, had unconsciously played out since early childhood. I realized that I had taken on the "family hero" role that my family so desperately needed me to play. As the minister and teacher who gave my family a public persona of success and proud accomplishment, I became the rock whom everyone expected to be strong and grounded. While many people looked up to me, I had no one with whom I could trust or share my feelings and needs, especially other men. Isolated and scared, I coped by being caustically sarcastic and superior.

Soon after this first awakening, my growth was given a rocket boost. In 1990 I attended a men's weekend retreat called the New Warrior Training Adventure where I was initiated into my healthier, soulful, unabashed maleness. Men invited me to become more authentic and to throw aside the roles, conditioning, and expectations that had been placed on me by my family and culture. During that journey, I discovered my own truths and my life's mission. Thus began the hard and abiding work of eliminating blocks within me that were preventing me from living my mission fully. On that weekend, newfound energy coursed through my body, heart, and soul. I found my passion and authenticity and discovered the power of working with a circle of men where there was safety, support, and healing.

When I met Leonard in our men's group, there was an instant connection and bond. As a fellow Midwesterner, writer, and facilitator, he felt like a brother from another mother. It became only a matter of time before we collaborated on writing this book. Leonard is this walking smile of a man with a huge heart, deep soul, and an unquenchable thirst for helping men heal. It was a writers' marriage made in heaven!

🔘 LEONARD AND RICK

We invite you to become the hero of your unfolding story and step through a threshold to embrace the quest to be a real man, one who embraces the heartfelt CLASSICS Model: Connection, Love, Authenticity, Spirituality, Sexuality, Intention, Community, and Sovereignty (kingship). Hop on board, strap on your seatbelt, and get ready for this adventurous ride into awakened manhood.

Chapter One

Calling Men into Wholeness

You can never change things by fighting the existing reality. To change something, build a new model that makes the existing model obsolete.

— R. Buckminster Fuller

A fifty-year-old man attended counseling with Leonard hoping to reconnect with his two children who were nineteen and twenty. They wanted nothing to do with him because he had divorced their mother five years earlier and abandoned them for his career. As he traveled around the world for his finance company, making millions of dollars, he spent little time with his children.

By all external measures, he was highly successful. Having bought into the old model of masculinity, however, he sat before Leonard a broken man. Though he had made more money than he knew how to spend, he had lost his relationship with his children and his connection with his heart and soul. He acknowledged that he had bankrupted their relationship and failed at fathering. He told Leonard that he had put more energy into making money than in loving his children but, in the process, felt unloved himself. If he had to do it over again, he would give up all his money to have a relationship with his children.

We have heard similar stories from many men. Believing our primary focus in life was to establish a career, make money, and be a provider, we have often neglected relationships with family, friends, and even ourselves. Success in the outer world defined us, rather than the quality of our relationships, both with ourselves and with others.

Now we are called to take another evolutionary leap to show up as men. If Neanderthal man hadn't evolved, we would probably be living in a cave, chewing on a saber-tooth tiger. Or perhaps, the tiger might be digesting us. Thank God, we continue to evolve.

When we speak of creating a blueprint of manhood, we by no means imply that we are defining the final model for masculinity. Quite the contrary: we are offering a blueprint that helps men continually evolve. We come from a generative universe where change and evolution are constant, ensuring the survival of the species.

From that place, we establish a paradigm to include the principle that since we are evolving, we can now consciously create how we want to show up as men. Our model invites men to move beyond what our culture deems as rigid roles. Conscious men support other men, women, children, and the planet.

But first, let's look at where we've come from and where we are now. Our ancestors once took on the role of hunter/warrior while women, because of their ability to bear children, adopted the role of gatherer/nurturer and healer. Men were expected to be powerful and successful hunters and provide for their family. As Aaron Kipnis wrote in *Knights Without Armor:*

"Hunting demanded the greater physical strength and endurance of the male body. Hunting also required the development of strong spatial skills. This allowed men to travel long distances without getting lost. It made them able to communicate the location of distant places to one another and to find their way home after days of wandering. Men's stronger hand-eye coordination and superior gross motor skills made bringing down the prey more likely. These are areas in which men still test higher today.

"Historically, women's superior verbal skills were needed to organize and catalog the many different foods, medicinal herbs, and plant materials that were collected. Their superior skills were needed for finding, collecting, preserving, and weaving. Women also required a more complex symbolic language to process this information and to transmit it to others. They required a more elaborate language for their work and childrearing. Gathering did not require women to remain silent at work."[3]

These roles shaped the identities of men and women through the ages. As humans evolved, men continued to perceive themselves as hunters and women as caregivers. During the Industrial Revolution, the social structure further reinforced "men's work" and "women's work," which established norms for male and female behavior. Men became the breadwinners while women became the bread-makers. Men protected the castle while the women tended the castle. These roles established a patriarchal society where men became the privileged gender with power, status, and control. This often contributed to violence.

James Gilligan, a psychiatrist who had been director of mental health for the Massachusetts prison system, wrote in *Violence: Reflections on a National Epidemic*, "Violence is primarily men's work; it is carried out more frequently against men; and it is about

---

3   Kipnis, Aaron, *Knights Without Armor*, Tarcher/Putnum, New York, 1991, pp 262-263.

the maintenance of 'manhood.'... Most of that violence, in every nation, every culture, and every continent in which it has been studied, and in every period of history, has always been violence by men against other men."[4] He does not minimize men's violence against women and says it is no less tragic, but far less frequent than the beatings and killings that men subject other men to. The role of women has often been to restrain the violence.

Gilligan goes on to state, "Violence—whatever else it might mean—is the ultimate means of communicating the absence of love by the person inflicting the violence."[5] Mass shootings may be the ultimate sign of that lack of love. In the United States, 98% of the 753 mass shootings in 2022 were perpetrated by men.

Movies today often depict men's heroic acts as occurring in combat. Violence is part of being a superhero to overcome evil, right a wrong, or seek justice. Manly acts become shoot-'em-up scenarios in video games and action thriller movies. Since aggression supposedly defines real men, characters like James Bond, Jason Bourne, Superman, Batman, and Wolverine present a model of manhood. The media still convey that message, whereas females hear a different one for themselves.

In a *New York Times* op-ed contribution by Michael Ian Black, he wrote,

"The past 50 years have redefined what it means to be female in America. Girls today are told they can do anything, be anyone. They've absorbed the message: they are outperforming in schools at every level. But it isn't about performance. To be a girl today is to be the beneficiary of decades of conversation about the complexities of womanhood, its many forms and expressions.

---

4   Gilligan, James, *Violence: Reflections on a National Epidemic*, Vintage Books, New York, 1997, pp. 6-7.

5   Ibid., p. 47.

"Boys, though, have been left behind. No commensurate movement has emerged to help them navigate toward a full expression of their gender. It's no longer enough to 'be a man' – we no longer know what it means.

"Too many boys are trapped in the same suffocating, outdated model of masculinity, where manhood is measured in strength, where there is no way to be vulnerable without being emasculated, where manliness is about having power over others. They are trapped, and they don't even have the language to talk about how they feel about being trapped, because the language that exists to discuss the full range of human emotions is still viewed as sensitive and feminine."[6]

Over the past century, we've seen dramatic shifts of roles, particularly with the advent of the feminist movement and now the #MeToo movement. As Terrence Real wrote in *The New Rules of Marriage*: "Women gained economic freedom, political power, a new psychology, and a collective drive to support feminine strength and independence.... In the last generation women have radically changed and men, by and large, have not."[7]

While many societies hope to achieve equality for women, a wide gap still exists between men and women in earning potential and positions of power. When this gap narrows, women's confidence and self-esteem may rise. But what happens to men?

In the eighth *Star Wars* movie, *The Last Jedi*, more women played roles as warriors, leaders, and decision-makers than in any previous *Star Wars* movie. Consider that the first movie in the series that appeared in 1977 portrayed Princes Leia as the lone female

---

6   Black, Michael Ian, "The Boys Are Not All Right," *New York Times* Op-Ed, Feb 21, 2018.

7   Real, Terrence, *The New Rules of Marriage: What You Need to Know to Make Marriage Work*, Ballantine Books, New York, 2007, p. 6.

heroic figure. *The Last Jedi* had plenty of women heroes. However, the villains, as in the first *Star Wars* movie forty years ago, were still mostly cast as men.

As women entered the corporate workplace, men started moving into the relational world of nurturing such as nursing, attending the births of their children, and becoming more active in caregiving. Changing tables for babies appeared in men's bathrooms, and paternity leave became instituted in some countries. However, since caregiving had no external rewards such as money and prestige, men were often taken to task in sitcoms about being bumbling partners and fathers. Who does society value more—an athlete who makes ten million dollars a year or a father who stays at home to care for his children? While we might respect the latter, most of us would admire the former. In our culture, external success and rewards trump relationships and inner peace.

RICK

My father was a successful salesman with a perpetual smile and a 'can do' attitude that permeated his existence. After his retirement, we spent five glorious days together camping and fishing in northern Wisconsin. Each morning, we'd get up with the sun, fish all day, then beach our boat to clean our catch and cook dinner. After dinner, we sat around a table near the fire and had precious talks.

"Okay, Rick," my father started, "you asked to spend time with me alone. What is it you want to know or hear?" To his credit, he listened carefully as I, at thirty-nine, explained my need to hear of his struggles, pain, and regrets.

He took a deep breath and dove into stories about his life—most of which I had never heard. He shared how difficult it was when his father died during the Depression. How his mother stepped up and cared for him and his brother, working two jobs, and about how he had given up his passion for music and college in order to go to work and help support his family.

He hesitated and then said, "Rick, I told you that I was fourteen years old when my dad died. Well, son, there's more to that story. At my father's funeral, my uncle came up to my mother and told her that she could not care for her two sons all by herself. He offered to take care of me until my mother got her feet under her. She agreed and sent me to live with my uncle for some time."

Then, very matter-of-factly, my father turned to me and said, "That was the first time my uncle had sex with me. This abuse went on for almost two years until my mother was able to take me back home. I have never told anyone about this, son. No one, until today."

I was stunned. With tears streaming down my eyes, I reached for my father's hand and peered into his eyes. "How did you deal with that huge wound all these years?"

He began to cry. "I did what men were taught to do back then. I pushed that event way deep down inside and never spoke of it again."

I took my father in my arms and held him as he sobbed out his pain, held in for over fifty years.

Some thirty-two years after his death, I still have tears over this memory. Despite his loving heart, my dad was engulfed in that old way of being a man, and, sadly, faced his trauma that way. He defined himself through his work and success and withstood unimaginable pain with toughness and control to protect his mother and my family.

In addition, my father was extremely competitive in the corporate world, working his way up the ladder to upper management. Suppression and avoidance stunted my father's emotional and spiritual growth. Like most men of his era, he had no other model to work from. I wonder if he would have lived a longer and more fulfilled life if he had been freed from the straitjacket of the rigid roles and principles about masculinity. Sadly, he died unexpectedly of heart failure three months after our fishing trip. I believe his heart could no longer carry the trauma any further, so his heart literally broke.

⦿ LEONARD

My father served in the Navy and was brought up in another era where vulnerability was equivalent to being unmanly. When he was released from a mental hospital after suffering a nervous breakdown, he carried tremendous shame. Men didn't have breakdowns, and if they did, they didn't talk about them.

My father would blame others, deny his problems, or minimize his own failures. In my father's eyes, acknowledging his own problems meant that he was less than a man. I experienced a few glimpses into his hidden life when he talked, albeit briefly, about serving in World War II when his ship was bombed. He lost buddies in battle but kept the details to himself. Bottling up his feelings, he protected himself with emotional armor. I did the same growing up.

Thankfully, the 21st century provides more choices and supports for us men; however, an underlying set of values and beliefs still propels us to maintain power and prestige. This old model of masculinity fosters the following principles for many of us:

1. A man and his success are defined by his career and work.

2. Real men are strong, aggressive, tough, powerful, and in control.

3. Competition over adversaries provides the road to success. Winning is equated with achievement while losing is equated with failure.

4. Feminine behavior should be avoided while masculine behavior must be reinforced.

5. Feelings that represent weakness, especially sadness, are for wimps and must be suppressed.

6. Vulnerability is to be avoided for it can be exploited by others.

7. Pain is part of being a man. Real men put up with physical discomfort and debilitating pain and don't complain, except to criticize others.

8. Because men are doers, men "fix" problems.

9. Real men are heterosexual and avoid behaviors that imply homosexuality.

10. A man's role is to take care of women—whether they need it or not.

Many of the ten principles still hold true for men. When Michael Ian Black wrote the "The Boys Are Not All Right" article, he posted it to his Twitter account. He received dozens of messages "impugning my manhood: the mildest of them called me a 'soy boy' (a common insult among the alt-right that links soy intake to estrogen)."[8]

Unfortunately, the old values and beliefs prevent us from living and relating authentically, which involves being vulnerable, sharing feelings, and creating cooperative partnerships. We are not suggesting, however, that we throw the baby boy out with the bath water. Quite the opposite. As Dr. Ronald Levant states, there are traits worth preserving and celebrating. He names seven of them in *A New Psychology of Men*[9]:

1. A man's willingness to set aside his own needs for the sake of his family

---

8   Black, Michael Ian, "The Boys Are Not All Right." *New York Times,* Feb. 22, 2018, Section A, Page 23.

9   Levant, Ronald and Pollack, William, *A New Psychology of Men*, Basic-Books, New York, 1995, p. 232.

2. His ability to withstand hardship and pain to protect others

3. His tendency to take care of people and solve their problems as if they were his own

4. His way of expressing love by doing things for others

5. His loyalty, dedication, and commitment

6. His stick-to-it-ive-ness and will to hang in until a situation is corrected

7. His abilities to solve problems, think logically, rely on himself, take risks, stay calm in the face of danger, and assert himself

The CLASSICS blueprint is about extending the range of masculine choices so that we can consciously choose how we want to be as men and how we want to grow. We can take the best values, beliefs, and behaviors from the old model while incorporating the CLASSICS traits. For example, there are times when we need to be tough and contain our feelings and times to be soft and express our emotions to loved ones. We do not have to be constrained by our biology, as some would have us believe.

It is true that men have significant differences from women in brain structures, chemical composition, and physical anatomy. The influence of environment, culture, and societal expectations creates a composite of current-day beliefs and expectations that establish gender roles, rules, values, and communication styles. However, these influences do not mean that culture and biology prevent us from evolving socially and personally. Otherwise, we become locked into the same argument that some women still battle today, that since their bodies are built to make babies, their primary role should be as caregivers.

Since we can alter our thinking, we can consciously participate in the evolution. We can choose how we want to define masculinity and create a different model for manhood. It merely requires us to discover and embrace those traits, principles, values, and beliefs that serve us. Once we define them, we can then begin to align our thoughts, feelings, and behaviors with a new vision of manhood.

That vision encompasses eight essential dimensions that help men thrive: **Connection, Love, Authenticity, Spirituality, Sexuality, Intention, Community, and Sovereignty.** Those eight characteristics will be fully explained in forthcoming chapters, but for now, let's summarize each one.

CONNECTION: VALUING EMOTIONS AND RELATIONSHIPS

I define connection as the energy that exists between people when they feel seen, heard, and valued; when they can give and receive without judgment; and when they derive sustenance and strength from the relationship.

— Brené Brown

The old model of manhood espoused toughness, rugged individualism, disconnection from feelings and bodies, and aggression to get ahead in the world. Men who are connected to emotions and relationships receives these benefits: a deeper understanding, appreciation, and love of self; more meaningful relationships; opportunities to satisfy emotional needs; increased vitality and vigor; greater capacity to establish and keep agreements; and a genuine desire for greater connection. In other words, we grow as men in connection, not in isolation.

LOVE: SHARING WITH AN OPEN HEART

Your task is not to seek for love but merely to seek and find all the barriers within yourself that you have built against it.

— *Rumi*

Love is as important to men as breath. However, we often feel more comfortable being warriors than lovers. Since love is inherent in each of us, we don't have to find it; we merely need to access it. That often involves finding and removing those barriers within ourselves that prevent us from giving and receiving love from a soulful place. We can then take steps to increase the power of self-love and love with an open heart.

AUTHENTICITY: RELATING VULNERABLY WITH ACCOUNTABILITY AND INTEGRITY

To be nobody-but-yourself—in a world which is doing its best, night and day, to make you somebody else—means to fight the hardest battle which any human being can fight; and never stop fighting.

— *e.e. cummings*

Being authentic means facing our fear of vulnerability and dropping our defensive armor. The price of not doing so takes a toll on our health and relationships. The Jungian concept of *shadow* illustrates how we hide disowned parts of ourselves. This book offers simple steps to be authentic and accountable to ourselves and others. Authenticity shines the light on integrity and accountability, key attributes for the evolving man.

SPIRITUALITY: CONNECTING WITHIN AND WITH OTHERS

Spirituality is recognizing and celebrating that we are all inextricably connected to each other by a power greater than all of us, and that our connection to that power and to one another is grounded in love and compassion.

— Brené Brown

Spirituality is different from religion. Religion attempts to codify and organize our connection with Spirit, while spirituality is the direct experience of Spirit that we feel in our hearts, minds, and souls. A connection to Spirit links us to something greater than ourselves. Our spiritual dimension guides us toward living a life of mission and purpose. We expand our spirituality through practices whereby we consciously connect to a Higher Power and, from that place, relate to others.

SEXUALITY: ACCESSING PLEASURE RESPONSIBLY

During the deepest sexual loving, you can feel so open, so full of light, so free of bounds, that you gasp, "Oh God!" and mean it.

— David Deida

Men are often uncomfortable having real conversations about their sexual selves, especially with other men. In the outmoded model, men postured, lied about sexual conquests, and magnified their imagined sexual power and potency even as they were completely mystified, terrified, and ignorant of their own sexual natures. When we open the door to a frank and honest discussion about our sexuality, we can let go of the shame and guilt, embrace that juicy part of ourselves, and sexually awaken as responsible men.

INTENTION: CREATING A MISSION OF SERVICE

Don't look for your dreams to become true; look to become true to your dreams.

— *Michael Beckwith*

For some, the word *intention* represents focusing on getting the right house, career, car, bank account, and partner. That form of intention can be ego-driven with the accumulation of objects as the prime objective. Success then becomes defined as attracting the right stuff. Our intention is to help men discover purpose and meaning in their lives. From that place, we consciously create a mission to utilize talents and skills to be of service. Mission is central to men living fully and making a lasting positive impact on others. In the process, we face and dissolve those shadow parts of ourselves that prevent us from realizing our vision and unleashing a powerful force on the world.

COMMUNITY: BUILDING A CIRCLE OF MEN

You may say I'm a dreamer, but I'm not the only one. I hope someday you'll join us. And the world will live as one.

— *John Lennon*

Community is a necessity in our ongoing evolution. Therefore, we need to feel connected to a brotherhood that helps us sustain our personal growth through the development and expansion of the eight dimensions. When we sit in a diverse circle with other men, we can share stories, acknowledge sorrows and victories, challenge old beliefs, and recognize and bless one another. Paradoxically, when men feel connected to other authentic men, we can more easily embrace women and children. Community offers a container to connect in love and authenticity to renew the mind, strengthen courage, and find heart.

SOVEREIGNTY: LEADING WITH YOUR INNER KING

When we are accessing the King energy correctly, as servants of our own inner King, we will manifest in our own lives the qualities of the good and rightful King, the King in his fullness.

— *Robert Moore & Douglas Gillette*

Sovereignty is about connecting with our inner authority, our wise King. If we were not raised in a proverbial castle with a wise King/ father figure, we may become a weakling or tyrant in our own kingdom. As men, we are called to harness the authority of our good King and integrate the inner advisors of the warrior, magician, and lover so we stand tall in the world.

As we expand our lives with these eight dimensions— Connection, Love, Authenticity, Spirituality, Sexuality, Intention, Community, and Sovereignty—we fully embrace the hero's quest. Join us as we step toward a healthier, evolving model of manhood.

STRETCHES

We include stretches after each chapter to expand and integrate the eight dimensions of masculinity with our mind, emotions, and spirits. A stretch in yoga allows our muscles to expand and strengthen. Similarly, these questions will expand your mind, emotions, heart, and soul. Sometimes, stretching feels uncomfortable. However, the discomfort can help you to wake up and show up stronger and more flexible.

The following questions will help you explore your current model of manhood.

1. What did your father and mother teach you about masculinity?

2. How did he and she relate to men, women, and children?

3. What would you have wanted from your parents, but never received?

4. Who were the significant males in your life, and what did they teach you?

5. Who are your current heroes? What attributes do these heroes exhibit?

6. If you could change one thing in your life, what would that be and how would you change it?

Chapter Two

Design Your Life: The Hero's Quest

After climbing a great hill, one only finds that there are many more hills to climb.

— Nelson Mandela

There's a legend about a farmer who plowed his field next to a majestic mountain. Every time he gazed at the mountain, he heard an inner voice calling him to climb. It was as if the Great Spirit of the mountain was summoning him to the top. He paid no attention to the call, thinking it a foolish quest. He much preferred the safety of his flat field and the security of his humble dwelling. But the call persisted: "Climb the mountain."

After many months of resisting, he finally mustered the courage to answer the call. He packed up his gear and started up the mountain. Along the way he stumbled and got hopelessly lost. He wandered aimlessly, despairing whether he would ever survive, let alone reach the top. But the Great Spirit of the mountain kept his hope alive, encouraging him to climb to the summit. Eventually, he found himself standing below the crest of the mountain. There, the Great Spirit beckoned him and reached down with a hand. The farmer grasped it and was pulled up to the top. He stretched his arms in gratitude and smiled at the Great Spirit who then pushed him off the mountain.

The farmer crashed down the mountain side and landed in his field, a broken man. Recovery took months. When he felt well, he heard that familiar call, "Climb, climb." Again, the farmer resisted, not wanting to endure another fall. However, the voice would not stop until he answered the call. This time he prepared himself for the climb with better provisions and a few companions. He enjoyed the vistas along the way, and with his companions' help, easily found his way to the top. There, the Great Spirit stood on the summit and again reached down to offer a hand. Remembering the crash, the farmer shook his head. "No, thanks. I'll do it on my own."

He climbed to the crest and stood with his arms stretched wide in gratitude, proud of his accomplishment. Feeling the wind beneath his arms, he smiled at the Great Spirit who smiled back and then pushed him down the mountain.

As the farmer fell, he cried out, "Why did you do this?"

The Great Spirit replied, "So you can spread your wings and fly."

The man spread his wings and flew.

This story exemplifies the hero's quest to climb a mountain. Like the legend, the quest involves four C's: Call, Climb, Crash, and Crest.

THE CALL

The call asks us to listen to a wake-up call and answer that inner voice which urges us to follow a dream, achieve a goal, heal our emotional wounds, redefine our life, connect with emotions, establish male friends, or fulfill a purpose. It asks us to leave behind the safety and security of the traditional roles and beliefs of manhood and take a leap of faith into a higher vision. Vision does not have a fear of heights. It is the road to growth and expansion where we, as men, gain strength and wisdom.

The old male model of suppressing emotions, being in control, and winning at all costs may have worked at one time, but we are entering a new age whose call expands and evolves our vision of masculinity to realize our true potential as men.

While all men are called to participate in this new undertaking, each of us will have a particular calling. The call may emanate from a wound that needs healing, a talent that needs expressing, a health challenge that plagues us, or a dream that must be fulfilled. Pain and pleasure are two forces that drive us up the mountain. We may be called to face an addiction, heal a broken relationship, or open our hearts to love and connection.

Wake-up calls are meant to point us in a direction to uncover the truth. They often begin as gentle reminders. However, if we rush around with frenetic lives and mental chatter, we don't hear the loving tap to get us moving. When we don't respond to the call but bury our head under a blanket, messages will come in increasingly dramatic fashion, such as traumas and personal crises. A partner may walk out, a life-threatening illness may strike, anxiety or despair may set in, or career and finances may be lost. Not surprisingly, when the pain of living becomes greater than the pain of change, we become motivated to change.

Crises generate heat for transformation. Consider the principle of thermodynamics. The Greek word for heat is *therme* while *dunamis* means power. Thermodynamics is the study of heat and its ability to bring about change. The Australian banksia tree produces a hard nut, the size of a large pinecone. To stimulate regeneration, the nut requires intense heat from a forest fire to release its seeds. No fire, no new trees.

The same principle applies to us. No wake-up calls, no transformation. Internal conflict creates dynamic heat. The energy cracks the window of an unconscious mind. Traumas open fissures in our psyche so eyes can turn inward, past the ruins of archaic masculine beliefs toward the beckoning heart of authentic connection.

In essence, the hero receives a call to adventure. Epic stories portray the hero as a man who rights a wrong, accomplishes amazing feats, discovers true love, battles inner demons, or radically changes his life. Should he fail to answer the call, he risks falling into a deeper hole of unconsciousness where he will remain until the next crisis which may show up as a bolt of lightning.

LEONARD

In July of 2004, I received one such call at two in the morning. My daughter, Melissa, phoned me from a hospital bed in Thailand. While she was riding on the back of a motorcycle on a rainy day, the bike had skidded on a bend in the highway. She was thrown to the pavement and hit by an oncoming car. Her hand was severely mangled. My ex-wife and I flew to Thailand and arranged for her to return to Chicago for multiple surgeries to repair lost tendons. Melissa's hand thankfully mended but not before turning her life and mine upside down.

At the time, I had a comfortable life with a private practice, scheduled time for writing, a lovely condo that overlooked a small lake in a Chicago suburb, and a wonderful group of friends. But something was missing. I had fallen asleep again and was meandering through life.

My daughter's wake-up call propelled me into a maelstrom. Knowing that I could have lost my daughter, I returned from Thailand with a burning desire to reignite the fire in my belly. I reviewed the facets of my life and took action. I joined a health club, signed up for yoga classes and personal growth seminars, shifted relationships, altered my attitude, and formulated a plan to relocate to California, which had been beckoning me for some time. Though I had traveled on and off the spiritual path throughout my life, my daughter's accident acted like a scorching forest fire that released the seed for a passionate embrace of the journey back Home. I have been committed to that path ever since.

Interestingly, Melissa's accident became her own wake-up call. It thrust her onto a course that led her to Australia to complete a nursing degree and a career path to help others. Crises offer poignant moments for reflection and evaluation.

I've received many other calls that were just as profound, like getting involved in men's work. That call came from my father wound as I needed to break out of being invisible and join the company of men who supported, encouraged, and challenged me to be "myself." Some calls I resisted, like finding my voice and expressing myself through writing. As a young boy and into adulthood, I kept receiving pens and pencils as gifts. Those calls irritated me. I wanted better presents than pens. I finally understood that I was called to break out of being invisible and express my heart and soul through writing and speaking.

RICK

Like Leonard and, I suspect, most of us, I have had many wake-up calls throughout my life. Some were developmental, like becoming a teacher, a minister, a husband, a father, a writer, and speaker. Others were deeply transformational, such as healing my inner child, pursuing my lifelong quest for spiritual awareness, and embracing shamanic healing and men's work. Some calls to wake up were agonizingly challenging and demanding. My two divorces and the loss of my son, though incredibly painful, pushed me to change dramatically! Those calls terrified me. Yet I would not be the man I am today if I had ignored them. In fact, I don't believe I would be alive today had I not responded to those calls which, in hindsight, became precious gems, offering amazing beauty when I take the time to polish their lessons. Without those calls, my life would be greatly diminished.

Though we are called, there is often a reluctance, even terror, to answer the call. We may have to endure a difficult climb, get pushed off our perch, and come crashing down to earth. If we avoid answering the calls, they will relentlessly pester us until we wake up and evolve. A health challenge or relationship breakup may rip us away from the comfort and security of the known world.

Leonard's friend, Hyder, had enjoyed it all: good health, happy marriage, beautiful daughter, comfortable home, wonderful community, and a great job. Then, out of the blue, his wife informed him that, after twenty years of marriage, she was leaving him. As he wrestled with the disaster, he received word that because of a corporate reorganization, his job was being dissolved. Then, to make his life even worse, he suffered a heart attack. He had hit the trifecta of wake-up calls summoning him to redesign his life. He knew that if he did not answer the call, he would receive another severe blow. Fearing that he would never be happy again, he reached out to a man in his men's group. He reminded Hyder of a poem by Hafiz, a Sufi poet; "Before a breakthrough, there is always a breakdown." That spurred him to create a legacy.

A wake-up call may push men to seek counseling or coaching. More often than not, they had repeatedly pushed the snooze button when they heard the alarm to change their lives. Only after a series of crises did they finally "get it" and seek help. A husband who was served divorce papers realized that his marriage was more important than golf or his job. He then actively sought marriage counseling. Unfortunately, it was too late for the relationship. However, the pain of losing his wife of fifteen years pushed him to work on himself and change the way he related to women.

The #MeToo movement has become a wake-up call of seismic proportions. The ground is moving beneath our feet. Women are exercising their voice to say "No" to sexual harassment and abuse. We are called to respond to the movement. Some men don't want to face the painful ramifications of harassment. However, we are called to raise our consciousness, evaluate our interactions with women, and take responsibility to correct abusive and sexist behaviors. In fact, we must even challenge other men when they become abusive.

Any call asks us to change our perspective. We may need to shift from despair to joy, powerlessness to power, codependency to self-care, fear to love, death to life, anxiety to peace, invisibility to visibility, disconnection to connection, and blame to self-responsibility. These shifts help us evolve.

One thing is certain. If we fail to answer the call, we will lead unfulfilled lives. However, when we finally commit to answer the call, we step into the next phase of the hero's journey. In fact, this book resulted from our, Leonard and Rick's, mutual call for us to help ourselves and other men evolve.

Consider these questions to clarify your call:

1. What are you currently called to do? (e.g., get in physical shape, pay off credit cards, attend a twelve-step group, write a book, expand a business, etc.)

2. What qualities are you called to develop? (e.g., trust, generosity, courage, creativity, compassion, self-love, etc.)

THE CLIMB

Climbing any mountain tests our perseverance, resilience, and inner strength. The climb asks us to face the fear of stepping out of our comfort zone into a new way of relating to the world as men. Taking on a climb forces us to grow our character.

The climb up any mountain involves treacherous ascents and descents. The climb down represents an inward journey to heal buried wounds. Robert Bly, author of *Iron John*, calls this stage, "Ashes work." Igniting passion is difficult when we have a fire pit filled with emotional ashes that need to be cleared. Therefore, we must descend to those places where we've buried suppressed anger, sadness, shame, or guilt that prevent us from ascending. As we clear out the ashes, we ascend past despair and loneliness toward fulfilling our mission and achieving our dreams on the mountain top. We're not meant to do this alone.

The old model of manhood portrayed climbing and success as a solo experience. The Marlboro man depicted a man on a horse, alone in rugged terrain, smoking a cigarette. Today, we're called to share the journey with other men. Having Sherpas, role models, and companions makes the climb easier and more rewarding. We can share our provisions and resources and laugh along the way to lighten the load. Role models point out what we haven't seen about ourselves, such as our isolation, lack of resources, and limiting beliefs, and either offer different perspectives or show quicker routes to get to the top.

If our fathers, who were meant to guide us toward manhood, were absent or ridiculing, we would have learned to mistrust men. Many of us have had to unlearn our fathers' lessons so that we could create a new vision of manhood. Associating with men of integrity helps us stay true to our path. They can also act as cheerleaders or as guard rails that stop us from slipping off the cliff.

Reacting to his horrific wake-up calls, Hyder talked to his friend about his loss of job, wife, and health. He received empathic support and wisdom to redesign his life and set a new destination. Hyder reviewed the road maps and books of others who overcame tragedies and climbed their own personal mountains. He faced his own obstacles of isolation and fear and reached out for the help of others so that he could share his climb, access the resource of love, gain wisdom, and strengthen his resolve to create his legacy.

Like all climbers, Hyder also needed to practice acceptance and letting go, crucial ingredients to any man's journey. Acceptance offsets any tendency to negatively judge ourselves. Most of us have received plenty of judgments since we were boys. For example, if we cried, we may have been judged as a wimp. Therefore, it's crucial that we practice acceptance on the climb, knowing that whatever we endured offered us experiences and wisdom. Recognizing where we are at, even if it feels horrible, takes courage. Rather than berating ourselves, we can accept our feelings and situations as part of the climb and then let go.

Letting go is rarely easy. Hanging onto a ledge prevents us from ascending the mountain. We may want to hold onto certain emotions such as resentment, anger, or grief, or we may want to hold onto toxic beliefs and behaviors, like controlling others. Letting go involves releasing the past so that we can live more fully in the present. It represents a shift in consciousness where we can forgive ourselves and those who have hurt us. As men, we may want to hold onto anger in an act of self-righteousness. Anger makes us feel powerful. Unfortunately, holding on merely keeps us stuck in a rut. Letting go allows us to reach for the next ledge on our climb up the mountain.

RICK

One of my most profound climbs occurred in 1990 when I completed my New Warrior Training Adventure initiation with sixty men, none of whom I had met previously. During that powerful weekend, the staff and my fellow participants supported me to get in touch with a raw vitality I had been lacking. I found my "wild man," an unabashed maleness that had been suppressed my entire life. I also discovered my mission. to create a passionately loving and peaceful planet by leading safe, sacred, diverse healing circles. Before that weekend, I had been a practitioner of Kriya Yoga for thirty years. I meditated every day for about an hour and attended my church four to five times a week. I was flying high with spirit, living mostly in the ethers, but not tethered to the earth. I found my earthy, wet, wild self on that weekend and wedded my spirit to my soul so instantly and so profoundly that it felt like 100,000 volts passing through my body. Transformed, I came off that weekend high on life, deeply connected to sixty men. That was a climb to remember!

LEONARD

Growing up, I learned to survive by being invisible. That kept me out of harm's way. Fortunately, many people showed up along the circuitous path up the mountain to lend me a hand. A nun in grammar school encouraged me to speak up in class. A Scoutmaster made me his assistant in the troop. College professors who inspired me during speech classes. A writing mentor who taught me to write.

Without their encouragement, I wouldn't have gained the confidence to express myself. During the climb I had to uncover suppressed emotions, heal past trauma, overcome the fear of speaking in front of groups, attend classes on writing and speaking, and learn communication skills to express my authentic voice.

What made the climb fun and rewarding were the mentors and fellow climbers who supported and guided me up the mountain. Without them, I would have given up the climb.

Consider these questions to make your climb easier:

1. What obstacles do you face as you climb your mountain?

2. What support do your need to make your climb easier?

THE CRASH

As it often happens with most heroic adventures, there is inevitably a dreaded crash. We may have faced a health issue, financial crisis, divorce, retrenchment, personal loss, addiction, or major failure. We can either be crushed by the crash or we can learn from it and develop character. Adversity forces us to review problems and failures, evaluate options, strengthen a positive attitude, and recommit to returning to the climb.

Failure is difficult for men because we have been taught that success defines manhood. While women have been viewed as sex objects, men are viewed as success objects. The greater the success, the bigger the man. Therefore, when a man crashes, so does his sense of self-worth.

The crash is when our inner hero can be truly born. We must decide to either drop our quest or return to it with greater conviction. During these times, we must face our failures—and we all have them. Only when we evaluate how we have failed or even faced the depths of despair can we move back up the mountain. The only failure is not learning a lesson. As Batman's father told him, "The purpose of falling is to get back up again."

When Hyder crashed, he had to overcome the dark emotional clouds of anger and fear. To catch a glimpse of sunshine, he sought the counsel of others and drew upon a practice outlined by Jack Kornfield in *Guided Meditations for Difficult Times: A Lamp in the Darkness*. The practice, like other similar visualizations, pictures the crash as an object. It can be represented as an enormous dark cushion that you're sitting on, a stormy cloud in the sky, or a crushing boulder that fell upon you. Using the power of imagination, you can alter the image to instill hope and empowerment. The cushion can shrink, the clouds can dissipate, and the boulder can be lifted by friends and tossed over the cliff.

Guided visualizations can help us through a crash. However, if the crash has been devastating, we need to seek other help. Unfortunately, men tend to suffer in silence rather than attend a support group or visit a doctor or therapist who could assist them. Shame can cripple us into the belief that we're unmanly because we are unable to tough it out. Going it alone when plummeting into a deep depression, overcoming prostate cancer, or filing bankruptcy creates isolation, loneliness, and despair. The new model encourages us to face failures, seek support, and evolve as men.

Both of us have heard countless stories from men who have crashed, learned from their experience, and made significant changes to improve their lives and show up differently. If it weren't for those crashes, they wouldn't have reached the top of the mountain. In fact, the crash made them more committed than ever to achieve happiness and satisfaction.

LEONARD

In the dead of a Chicago winter in 1991, I walked aimlessly in tears around the neighborhood in icy rain. I had recently moved back to Chicago after spending fourteen wonderful years in Australia. Marylou, my wife at the time, needed to return to Chicago so that she and our two children could spend more time with family. I vehemently resisted the move as I had made Australia my home. However, Marylou was adamant about returning to be near her family. So, I joined her in the move, leaving behind sunny Australia, my private practice, friends, and status.

Regrettably, I brought along my resentment about returning to Chicago. I discovered that I suffered from Seasonal Affective Disorder where lack of sunlight impacts mood. Without the sun in the bitter winters, Chicago became an unwelcome place. I had to find a job, but since I had given up my Illinois therapy license, believing I would make Australia my home, I had to study for and take another examination. In the meantime, I worked some construction jobs for my brother to bring in money. As I walked the streets of Chicago in the freezing rain, I faced all that I had lost. What became most difficult was the loss of my partner as we headed for divorce. I tumbled onto the rocks of depression, loneliness, and inadequacy, a broken man.

The crash, however, forced me to face my situation. I could either squander my life or start climbing again. Thankfully, I found a band of brothers who were there to support me through my healing. I became part of a men's group that lasted seventeen years in Chicago. I attended the New Warrior Training Adventure and, later, the Men's Room weekend. They solidified my journey toward real manhood. I realized that climbing buddies were necessary if I ever wanted to reach the top of the mountain. Thank God, I found them.

RICK

Undoubtedly, my most impactful crash occurred at the end of my first marriage, in 2002. In short order, my then-wife falsely accused me of sexually assaulting our oldest daughter, left with my other daughter, and got involved with another man. We later filed for divorce, but in a flash, I lost my marriage, much of the relationship with my daughters, my home, and I came close to losing my freedom and my thirty-year teaching career. A major crash, indeed! To say I was stunned, depressed, grief-stricken, and angry is an understatement. Like the man whom God threw off the mountain in the story that begins this chapter, I was bruised, battered, bloodied, and broken.

Men's groups offer a nurturing place where we can talk honestly about parts of our lives that are not going well, for example, crashing into an addiction, self-sabotage, divorce, or despair. It doesn't matter what the problem is; it only matters that we talk about our problems. In our model, we communicate our feelings and our failures.

Consider these questions to gain perspective about a crash:

1. Describe a recent crash and how you handled it.

2. What lessons or gifts did you receive from that crash?

THE CREST

The final part of the journey takes us to the crest. That place asks us to celebrate the victory of a difficult climb with gratitude. We must savor the view and relish our accomplishments and recognize the grand purpose of the journey with its twists and turns. The crest is a time to recognize the life lessons that became the gold that we accumulated along the way. In men's work, gold represents the talents, gifts, lessons, and self-love and appreciation that define who and where we are.

Celebrations can occur along the road for minor victories like a week of sobriety or they can happen with major victories like ten years of sobriety. Men's groups honor the commitments of others and acknowledge their accountability and integrity.

The crest does have its dark side. Phil Jackson, coach of the Chicago Bulls and the Los Angeles Lakers, wrote in his book, *Sacred Hoops: Spiritual Lessons of a Hardwood Warrior,* "Success tends to distort reality and make everybody, coaches as well as players, forget their shortcomings and exaggerate their contributions. Soon they begin to lose sight of what made them successful in the first place: their connection with each other as a team." He then quotes Michael Jordan, "Success turns we's back into me's."[10]

We have met successful men who became arrogant and condescending toward others who were unable to reach the crest. Rather than help, they ridiculed those less fortunate and called them losers. The crest offers rewards. We are not meant to squander them.

The final phase of the heroic mountain climb is the telling of our defeats and victories. That's what happened around the campfire with our ancestors. Our lessons, morals, and insights are viewed from a higher place of wisdom and integration that inspires other men to share their stories. From that higher perspective we bless other men who climbed their own mountains.

10   Jackson, Phil and Delehanty, Hugh, *Sacred Hoops: Spiritual Lessons of a Hardwood Warrior,* Hyperion, New York, 1995, p. 156.

Hyder Zahed celebrated his crest by incorporating all the lessons from his call, climb, and crash into a book published in 2013, *Create Your Legacy: Four Portals to Living a Life of Love and Caring*. Through his book and workshops, he passed on all that he learned so that others could have an easier climb.

RICK

Just as I've had many crashes, I have also experienced amazing crests. I know I could not have reached these summits, nor have felt as fulfilled without the crucial and loving support from many men in my life, including a longtime men's circle in Milwaukee during my divorce saga. Those beautiful men stepped up in unimaginable ways to love and support me through that trying time. They regularly reminded me of the truth of who I was. They offered their homes, helped me move, offered money to find myself a lawyer, and gave so much support. Honestly, I do not know if I could have survived such a stunning and unspeakably painful crash without their unconditional support. I am forever grateful.

I've shared this story many times with circles of men, mostly as therapy for me, but also to glean wisdom from the crash. Even so, virtually every time I have told this story, one or more men have come forward to relate their own version of a similar tale, and to thank me for having the courage to share my crash so they could revisit and integrate the lessons into their lives.

LEONARD

I've had the good fortune to have reached many crests. Raising two children has been one of the hardest things I have ever done in my life, so I feel quite proud to see Melissa and Nate as incredible human beings who also have wonderful families and careers. I'm also proud of the fact that I persevered over the years through many rejections

(130 for my first book) and setbacks to have four books published. That includes two novels and two self-help books, one of which was co-authored with my friend, Mari Frank. Each book represented a mountain in and of itself.

I'm also proud of the fact that I've taken many risks in life, like moving to Australia and at the age of sixty, starting over in California. Those vistas from the top look sweet. However, the one crest that makes me beam is where I'm now at in life. Having turned seventy-two, I am ever so grateful for all the journeys I've taken and even the crashes, for they brought incredible lessons and gifts. On top of my crest, I rejoice that I made it. Thank God, there are more mountains to climb. Hooray!

Once achieved, we're not meant to just stand on the crest. We're asked to fly off the mountain and inspire other men to climb their mountains.

Consider these questions to gain perspective of your crest:

1. Name one of your heroic climbs, victories, or accomplishments. What did you learn?

2. How did you celebrate your victory?

STRETCHES TO CLIMB
YOUR MOUNTAIN

THE CALL

1. What mountain are you called to climb?

2. How do you want to feel when you reach the top?

3. How do you resist the call?

THE CLIMB

1. What resources or talents do you bring to the climb?

2. Who can you call on for help?

3. What qualities do you want in a mentor or climbing buddies?

THE CRASH

1. How do you usually handle crashes in your life?

2. How do you ask for help?

3. What could you do differently the next time you crash?

THE CREST

1. If you stood on the top of your mountain, what would that feel and look like?

2. How does that perspective change the way you see the world?

3. How can you help others reach their crests?

Chapter Three

Build a Life of Connection

I define connection as the energy that exists between people when they feel seen, heard, and valued; when they can give and receive without judgment; and when they derive sustenance and strength from the relationship.

— *Brené Brown*

I n his first therapy session with Leonard, Phil complained of being anxious and depressed. These feelings baffled and frustrated him because he was normally upbeat and energetic. He prided himself on being an excellent manager at his office, but his work was now suffering. Responding to his wife's constant requests that he seek help, he finally made an appointment.

During the interview, Phil spoke impassively about the fact that several months earlier, he'd found his twenty-six-year-old son hanging in his garage. The suicide of his only son weighed heavily, but Phil believed he had to remain strong for his wife and daughter. During the session, Phil's face tensed as he struggled to choke down the grief. He had been taught by his father to act like a man, so much so that if Phil cried as a boy, he was taken to the shed and beaten. Expressing sadness was for women, not for men.

Clutching his father's beliefs, Phil had built his life around the old model of manhood. As he proudly said, "If you lop off one of my legs, I won't flinch, and even if you cut off my other leg, I'll show you that I can take it."

He was prepared to hold onto the grief that weighed heavy on his heart. Disconnected from feelings, he distanced himself from his family and his coworkers. The depression and anxiety acted as a wake-up call to face the devastation in his life and climb the mountain of connection. He had to learn, in the company of another man—his therapist—that connecting with emotions was far from shameful and that clutching painful emotions stifled energy and created bitterness and resentment. However, getting in touch with feelings required courage and made him whole rather than half a man.

During the course of therapy, Phil finally got the message when he heard two metaphors. The first had to do with drinking and peeing. When he consumed water, eventually he had to release it. If not, his bladder would experience discomfort and pain. Holding onto grief was like holding onto urine. He could either go numb from the pain and become more depressed and cut off from his relationships, or learn to let go and experience sweet relief.

The second metaphor focused on the process of forging a sword. That occurs when the blade is repeatedly placed in a fire and tempered so that it could be strong. Sadness and grief represented fire to soften and forge a whole man. One needed courage to enter those fiery emotions and be tempered by compassion and love.

With Leonard's support, Phil decided to enter the healing cauldron where his unexpressed emotions that boiled beneath the surface bubbled upward into consciousness. He softened and wept, not only for his son, but for all the painful years of his childhood. He answered the call and climbed, sometimes stumbling up the mountain and crashing, but he always returned to the climb of connection. He faced painful emotions, including guilt about imparting his beliefs about toughness onto his son and feeling powerless about stopping his son's suicide. At one session he refused to use the tissues and pulled out a bandanna which he called a real man's handkerchief. He wept into that bandanna.

In a session that included his wife and daughter, he shared more of his feelings, prompting the family to grieve together. They later shared tears of joy that Phil was showing up as a loving man more connected to his family.

In our experience, Phil wasn't alone in his belief that men should not express feelings of vulnerability, like grief, shame, or guilt. We were taught to build walls of invulnerability. However, as Patricia Albere, founder of the Evolutionary Collective, wrote, "The more we felt threatened, abandoned, or insecure as babies and young children, the more likely it is that our ego structure will develop in ways that encase us in thick, defensive walls of fixed ideas, images, and rigid beliefs…. Then, openness and vulnerability will seem dangerous and unwise, and we will be too afraid to be shaped by outside influences."[11]

Most men dread vulnerability and see it as a weakness. Being vulnerable and expressing tenderhearted feelings have been relegated to the realm of the feminine, and any man who acted feminine would be considered weak or gay. Men have shamed other men who expressed emotions with the berating statement, "Don't be a pussy!" Being called a *pussy* for acting in ways that appeared feminine not only demeaned men, but also women, as if female genitalia was weak or evil.

In his book, *I Don't Want to Talk About It*, Terrence Real describes a study where researchers, Hammen and Peters, tested hundreds of college roommates on the same issue. "They found

---

11   Albere, Patricia, *Evolutionary Relationships: Unleashing the Power of Mutual Awakening*, Oracle Institute Pres, Independence, VA, 2017, p. 150.

that when female college students reached out to their roommates for support about being depressed, they met with nurturing and caring reactions. In contrast, when male students disclosed depression to their roommates, they were met with social isolation and often with outright hostility. The 'roommate study' was later repeated on campuses all over the country with much the same results."[12]

This research highlights how we are reluctant to reach out and connect, especially when feeling anxious, depressed, or stressed. No wonder we disconnect from our emotions and relationships when we become overwhelmed and feel vulnerable.

RICK

My childhood is riddled with situations where I was discounted and shamed. These feelings were most present when I was eight years old. My family left the Catholic Church and joined a church of yoga called Self Realization Fellowship. In Milwaukee in the 1950s, this change was beyond weird! I became a vegetarian, stopped attending Catholic school, stopped reading the Bible, and moved to a public school.

I wasn't fully aware how unusual this situation was until my friends stopped coming to my house or inviting me to theirs. Because I was no longer Christian, I lost most of my friends. At Cub Scout campouts, I faced ridicule from the other scouts, like when I roasted my vegetarian soybean hot dog over the campfire and it broke in half, landing in the fire. Then my parents split, and I moved to the inner city of Milwaukee, Wisconsin, with my mother and siblings.

I had no friends, no allies, and my sibs and parents were lost in their own trauma. I never felt so scared and alone. At eight years old, I had already put on my armor. I learned to cover and hide my religion and my vulnerable self from people. Acting tough and playing

---

12   Real, Terrence, *I Don't Want to Talk About It: Overcoming the Secret Legacy of Male Depression*, Scribner, New York, 1997 p. 38.

competitively with other boys gave me comfort and status. I went into survival mode.

Every beating from my classmates and every betrayal, abandonment, or dismissal hardened my armor and deepened my persona of invulnerability. I covered my shame by becoming an obnoxious know-it-all and got some status in school by being funny and painfully sarcastic. I was completely disconnected. It wasn't until thirty years later, when my dysfunctional coping behaviors were no longer working, and my marriage and family were terrifyingly at risk, that I painfully began the process of peeling off my thick layer of armor. That process continues to this day. My armor is now permeable, but still necessary at times. I am more conscious of when I put it on and when I can take it off.

Peeling off protective layers is not easy, as the old model of manhood espouses toughness, rugged individualism, and aggression to get ahead in the world. Surviving and competing with other men meant armoring ourselves and not letting down our guard lest we be attacked. Most of us learned this from our fathers.

Our fathers' values often espoused competitiveness, aggressiveness, independence, separateness, self-sufficiency, toughness, invulnerability, and non-emotionality. Fathers who were emotionally or physically unavailable modeled disconnection. We, as boys, learned to suppress feelings that were not deemed appropriate and adopted the belief, "Boys don't cry."

◕ LEONARD

When my son, Nate, was eleven years old and we lived in Australia, he was playing on the rugby team in his sixth grade. Playing against a very tough opponent, Nate and his teammates were getting clobbered. One of the boys fell to the ground after a clash and started crying. I overheard one of the fathers say, "Give 'em time, and he won't feel a thing."

If we express sadness, we are often shamed. Consider Jayson, a 28-year-old man who came to Leonard for counseling after his wife left him and their 8-year-old marriage for another man. Like many men, Jayson felt emotionally isolated and ashamed of his grief. He had turned to his father for support, but rather than getting empathy or compassion, he received an angry barrage. "Don't be a pussy," stormed his father. "You're crying like a baby. Get over it and find another woman!"

Like Jayson and the Aussie boy, we are taught to "not feel a thing" and steel ourselves against pain. No talking, no feeling, no crying, no sign of a whimper—even if we're kicked to the ground. We are supposed to suppress our feelings and, above all, tell no one about the depth of our pain. Just move on till no more can be endured—then collapse. After all, isn't that what men are all about! Ask any athlete who risks serious injury to his body by ignoring the pain and playing through it.

There's a fine line between courage and stupidity. Our emotions and senses connect us to our internal world. They provide feedback so that we can relate to the world. If we disconnect from some of our emotions and physical senses, we, in effect, shut down our feedback system. Imagine a red light appearing on the dashboard of a car indicating a malfunction but, instead of addressing the call to action, we place duct tape over the dashboard. That's what happens when we stop paying attention to our emotions.

🕛 LEONARD

Many years ago, I provided crisis counseling to the staff of a major department store in Chicago. A beloved employee had been murdered, and management wisely offered the staff an opportunity to talk about their grief. They provided a group session for the employees. Twenty-six women showed up to deal with their pain over the loss of their coworker who had worked in the store for twenty-four years and had become a friend to many. At one point, a couple of men walked in and glanced around at the women, many of whom were crying. Not wanting to connect with their emotions, they bolted from the room. If they had been open, they would have been able to give and receive support, move through their emotions, and feel more connected to their fellow employees.

Whenever we disconnect from our feelings and senses such as pain or discomfort or even pleasure, we stop ourselves from being fully present. If we bury emotional wounds suffered through trauma, we risk going numb and detaching from feelings and relationships. Connection to self and others keeps us alive and vibrant.

Our body is an intelligent organism that talks to us daily and offers guidance. If we experience pain, our body sends us messages to take corrective measures. Ilchi Lee wrote in *Human Technology: A Toolkit for Authentic Living*, "When we are sensitive and responsive to the signs and rhythms of our body, we are more deeply connected to the rich, wonderful texture of all life experience."[13] Heightened senses lead us to elevated states of pleasure, even bliss. Who wouldn't want to experience such states?

Emotional intelligence is about becoming aware of our wide range of emotions and learning about expressing and managing them. At the same time, being emotionally intelligent in relationships allows us to empathize with others and manage our interactions.

While we obviously want to feel joy and love, it's important to realize that all emotions such as sadness, fear, and anger help us identify needs, wants, and desires and move us toward action

---

13   Lee, Ilchi, *Human Technology: A Toolkit for Authentic Living*, Healing Society, Sedona, AZ, 2005, p. 20.

in healthier ways. Discordant emotions alert us to problems and harmonious ones lead us to inner peace.

Our five main feelings are anger (mad), grief (sad), fear (scared), shame (I'm defective), and joy (glad). Each of them can help us build an emotionally balanced and centered life. Here are some ways we can use each emotion as a power tool.

When we feel angry, we can ask ourselves, "What boundary has been crossed? What agreement has been broken?" Anger may call us to access the inner warrior to defend or reset our boundaries.

When we feel sad, we can ask ourselves, "What have I lost? What am I grieving?" Sadness offers us an opportunity to acknowledge and honor any losses. Releasing tears can be cleansing and can even teach us about compassion for others who suffer.

When we are afraid, we might ask ourselves, "What am I scared of? What is my worst fear about this situation?" Without fear, we cannot build our courage muscle because it takes courage to face fear and step through it.

When we feel shamed, we might ask ourselves, "What part of me feels judged, defective, or not good enough?" If we share our shame with someone we trust, deep healing from childhood wounds can occur.

When we feel joy, we can ask ourselves, "What am I experiencing or doing that brings me joy? How long can I experience joy?" Such an awareness reminds us to keep on doing that which brings us joy.

The mystic Rumi knew about the power tools of emotions. He aptly describes them in his poem, "The Guest House."

This being human is a guest house
Every morning a new arrival.
A joy, a depression, a meanness,
some momentary awareness comes
as an unexpected visitor.

Welcome and entertain them all!
Even if they are a crowd of sorrows,
who violently sweep your house
empty of its furniture,
still treat each guest honorably.
He may be clearing you out for some new delight.
The dark thought, the shame, the malice,
meet them at the door laughing,
and invite them in.
Be grateful for whoever comes,
because each has been sent
as a guide from beyond.

The interplay of opposites assists us to fly, as suggested in another of poem by Rumi: "God turns you from one feeling to another, and teaches by means of opposites, so that you have two wings to fly, not one." Without fear, we don't experience courage. Without sorrow, we don't fully embrace gratitude. Without anxiety or worry, we don't appreciate ease and contentment. Loss can teach us to appreciate what we have.

Each emotion, like a color on a painter's palette or life's canvas, offers contrast. An artist can utilize hues of reds, blues, and yellows to create a richly textured picture. Emotions are the colors on life's canvas. Young children express themselves freely. When upset, they cry and when happy, smile or laugh. Boys are taught not to paint with tears; girls not to use anger. Growing up, men are encouraged to fight the good fight in competitive sports, business, or war. However, fighting often means that we suppress sadness, shame, guilt, and fear. Suppressed emotions stifle energy and creativity and lead to depression and anxiety. When we deny our feelings, we cause them to go underground to ferment and expand until they find an alternative form of expression, sometimes in the form of violence.

🌑 LEONARD

As a child, I suppressed truckloads of sadness and anger. The family's coping mechanism for handling emotional pain was to get busy. That didn't always work for me, especially if my father berated me on one of my Sunday visits to his apartment. To vent my anger, I would get into fights with my older brother. The scars on my head are a permanent record of our many punch-ups. Back then, my brother and I never talked about my dad's mental illness or his abandoning the family. Had we dealt with our emotions, we could have faced tears rather than fists.

DAVID HEIMAN (Long-time member of our men's group)

I had a big disconnect many years ago between my heart and my head. I had everything compartmentalized in my life. I placed friends in one corner, work in one place, and family in another. Living that way wasn't serving me or anyone else. I sought to increase the connection between my head and heart. Men's work was that avenue for me. Today I am blessed and grateful that I get to live in connection with my head and heart, and with other men who have that same connection, who freely and openly express their emotions. Whatever I'm feeling, it's okay to show it, whether I'm angry, sad, joyful, happy, fearful, or shameful. My life has changed radically for the better.

Using our emotions as power tools does not mean we have license to infringe on others' rights. If we're angry, we can't just smack someone. We connect with our emotions intelligently when we acknowledge our feelings without judgment and process them to increase self-understanding. That means expressing emotions appropriately with others.

Consider Ralph whose wife left him after three years of marriage. At twenty-eight, he lost the woman of his dreams. She complained about his inability to express himself emotionally. She wanted a man who was passionate, and, after finding one, she ended the marriage.

His depression was evident. Ralph had difficulty sleeping and eating and could not focus on his job. He was taking antidepressant medication from a psychiatrist but reported that he did not feel any better. He was completely shut down and didn't feel a thing.

During a counseling session, Leonard walked him through a list of six questions to help him get in touch with his emotions. He was told that there were no right or wrong answers and that he was to avoid attacking, defending, or judging himself.

1. What are you feeling? Give yourself permission to acknowledge any anger, fear, shame, or sadness.

2. What triggered that feeling? Name what happened.

3. Where do you feel that emotion in your body? (e.g., gut, chest, head, etc.) Give it a color, shape, and texture. (e.g., a black rock in my gut.)

4. If that shape or emotion had a voice, what would it say?

5. What does the emotion need or want?

6. What can you do now to satisfy that need? (e.g., share your feelings with others.)

After being encouraged to relax and let go of any expectations, he followed Leonard's instructions to deepen his relaxation with deep breaths. He was then asked to share what he was experiencing and to let his body speak. Initially, he had difficulty connecting with any emotion but settled on sadness. When asked to imagine a place where the sadness might reside, he mentioned his chest and throat as places where he tensed up when stressed. He then described the tension as a large, sharp, gray rock.

Leonard asked him to give the rock a voice. At first, there was silence, then the rock whispered, "I miss my wife."

With encouragement, Ralph, ever so slowly, allowed the rock to speak. Giving voice to the rock, he unlocked a room full of grief. He began to sob at the loss of his wife who had been his only friend. He cried about the pain in his chest and throat as he shared feelings never expressed. He longed to be with her and blamed himself for pushing her away.

After going through a box of tissues, he experienced relief. He realized that he needed to let go of his pain and self-blame; otherwise, they would eat him alive. He made a commitment to connect more with his feelings and express them.

Being willing to let painful feelings go sets up a chain reaction to move through the emotions and allow others to emerge, like forgiveness and even gratitude. If we hold onto painful emotions, we need to ask ourselves if there is a payoff to holding onto these feelings. This hidden motivation may be hard to spot. However, when we hold onto anger or resentment, there is usually some reward and a cost. The supposed payoff may be feeling self-righteous or avoiding conflict. The cost of holding onto pain may lead to emotional and physical illness.

Candace Pert, a neuropharmacologist, shows through her research how the human body stores emotions. When suppressed, they impact the immune systems and cause a host of problems. In *Molecules of Emotion: Why You Feel the Way You Feel*, she writes, "Anger, grief, fear—these emotional experiences are not negative in themselves; in fact, they are vital for our survival. We need anger to define boundaries, grief to deal with our losses, and fear to protect ourselves from danger. It's only when these feelings are denied, so that they cannot be easily and rapidly processed through the system and released, that the situation becomes toxic... the more we deny them, the greater the ultimate toxicity, which often takes the form of an explosive release of pent-up emotions. That's when emotion can be damaging to both oneself and others, because its expression becomes overwhelming, sometimes even violent "[14]

With consistent practice, using the power tool of connecting with emotions and expressing them becomes easier. Over time, you develop a deeper understanding, appreciation, and love of self. You acknowledge your needs and satisfy them, and you foster more meaningful relationships. When you connect with other men who are on the same program, you will further your awareness and deepen your skill set.

RICK

Gabe, a Viet Nam combat vet, attended a veteran's healing workshop that I facilitated. Stooped over, he barely looked at the other men in the circle. He had spent years volunteering on staff for a program called "The Vets' Journey Home," dedicated to helping veterans heal from trauma. While Gabe had tirelessly assisted other vets to heal and take back their hearts and souls, he had not done his own work.

I connected almost immediately with him and instinctively knew that Gabe's secret was about his combat experience. I also knew that Gabe would process his trauma only when he felt safe.

One Saturday afternoon, Gabe took a risk and asked me to work with him in the group. He said, "I don't know if I can share this secret, but I know I must. I have been carrying it for thirty-eight years. It's killing me and keeping me from being the husband, dad, and friend I want to be. I've been depressed and suicidal for years. My secret is so painful that I can't share it out loud."

At first, I just listened. I then asked, "Do you trust me enough to whisper your shame into my ear?"

---

14   Pert, Candace, *Molecules of Emotion: Why You Feel the Way You Feel,* Scribner, New York, 1997, pp. 285-286.

He considered that request for a moment. He nodded with tears in his eyes. "Yes, I do."

He leaned close to my ear and said, ever so softly, "I killed a Vietnamese soldier in hand-to-hand combat in 1975. I sliced his throat." He began to sob. "I held this enemy while the life ebbed out of him. As he died, I looked into his eyes and realized he wasn't evil. He wasn't my enemy. He was just like me, fighting to protect his country and family."

He continued in a whisper, "At that moment, I felt intense shame and regret. I had to shut down my heart and soul. I hated myself for my violent act. In my head, I knew I had done my duty, and I was glad I survived, but I could not forgive myself for ending another man's life. It was as if I had died that day. Carrying this around is killing me. It feels as if I walk around in a black cloud. How can I forgive myself?"

I told Gabe that shame is about secrets. Sharing the secret with others who can hear and love you is a powerful way to heal and forgive yourself. I asked him what he needed.

"My God, that is hard to say. I need to know you will accept me even though you know this horrible thing. I am afraid you and others will judge me or leave me when you find out the truth."

Tears trickled down my cheeks as I looked into Gabe's eyes. "You may not believe this, but I love you and accept you more now that you have shared your secret."

Gabe then asked me if I would help him share this secret with the other men. "I need to do this. My heart's thawing!"

I had Gabe choose a man whom he trusted to hold his secret and share it with him. He then whispered his secret into that man's ears. Both men cried as the other man revealed that he'd also killed men in battle.

With newfound courage, Gabe spoke to the whole group about his secret. In the process, he received acceptance and love from the other men. However, there was one other man who needed to shower Gabe with acceptance and love.

I found a mirror and placed it in front of him. "Look at the man in the mirror. Share your secret and ask him to love and accept you."

Gabe hesitated before looking at his reflection. He stood ramrod straight and said, "I killed a man in combat. Do you still love me and accept me?"

"How does the man in the mirror respond?"

"I forgive you," he said to his reflection. "I've waited a long time for forgiveness. I didn't know it had to come from inside. You are a good man, Gabe!"

The circle of men surrounded him. "You are a good man—and loved!"

I kept in contact with Gabe for some time after that event and staffed with him on another training. His transformation continued as his depression lifted, and his relationship with his wife and kids blossomed.

Emotional connection bridges relationships. In fact, it is the glue in relationships. After sharing intimate feelings with another, we feel closer. And if we resolve conflict together successfully, we're drawn into a closer bond.

We may feel comfortable standing shoulder-to-shoulder with another man—the buddy system. However, to experience another man, face to face, can be perceived as an invitation to confrontation, possibly leading to disconnection or even physical withdrawal or violence. To grow and develop as men, we need that face-to-face connection, where we break out of isolation and deal directly, in a non-competitive manner with others.

In summary, the benefits of using the power tool of connecting in relationships are numerous: a deeper understanding, appreciation, and love of self; more meaningful relationships; opportunities to satisfy emotional needs; increased vitality and vigor; greater capacity to establish and keep agreements; and a genuine desire for greater connection. In other words, we grow as men in relationships.

The following steps help us connect in relationships:

- We willingly increase our awareness of what we are feeling or sensing in the present moment and acknowledge them without judgment.

- We desire to connect and create space without interruption that allows vulnerability, understanding, and empathy.

- We share our experiences, whatever arises, whether they be emotions or senses, face to face, with another person.

- We mutually listen to, encourage, and support one another to be open and vulnerable.

- We ask for what we need in relationships and consider the other person's needs.

- We stay committed to the ongoing process of connection and nourish and strengthen the connection as an entity in itself, the we-ness.

We establish an attachment to others when we reveal our senses, emotions, and thoughts, and listen to others. We may notice similarities as well as differences, but as we reduce separation and move closer emotionally, we develop deep connectivity.

Sometimes we may feel the need to withdraw into our caves so that we can reconnect with ourselves and recognize thoughts and feelings. Once grounded, we can then re-emerge into the world as more evolved men. Connection is about balancing the flow between self and another.

Deepening the connection implies an emerging awareness of our inner and outer worlds. Connection replenishes and revitalizes, like inhaling and exhaling air. From that place, we embrace the breath of life—**Love,** the next dimension of our CLASSICS model.

STRETCH YOUR EMOTIONS AND RELATIONSHIPS

1. What emotions do you feel comfortable and uncomfortable expressing?

2. What makes you mad?

   a. When you are mad, what do you usually do? How would you like to express anger?

3. What makes you sad?

   a. When you are sad, what do you usually do? How would you like to express sadness?

4. What makes you scared?

   a. When you are scared, what do you usually do? How would you like to express fear?

5. What makes you feel ashamed?

   a. When you feel ashamed, how do you express that feeling? How would you like to express your shame and heal from it?

6. What makes you feel joy?

   a. When you feel joy, how do you express that emotion? How would you like to express joy?

7.   What makes you feel loved?

    a.   When you feel loved, how do you express that feeling? How would you like to express love?

8.   Think of a relationship where you feel disconnected but want to connect. What can you do to reconnect with that person? (For example, share your desire to be close, talk about your feelings, etc.)

Chapter Four

Build a Life of Love

*Your task is not to seek for love but merely to seek
and find all the barriers within yourself you have
built against it.*

— Rumi

Men have difficulty with three powerful words—I love you.
We may demonstrate our love for a partner or our children through action, or we may tell a close male friend in
an off-handed way, "Luv you, Bro." But dropping our armor and
opening our heart can feel quite threatening.

Men have been socialized to associate masculinity with power,
strength, toughness, and achievement—the realm of the warrior.
While these qualities help us survive and succeed in a competitive
environment, they are not the qualities that build intimate relationships. Love requires openness, vulnerability, sensitivity, compassion,
and emotional availability—qualities that are often perceived as
feminine. If a man embraces those qualities, he may be shamed by
other men as being feminine or gay.

Therefore, entering the domain of the lover means dropping
the armor and becoming emotionally vulnerable. That raises a host
of fears: rejection, abandonment, smothering, becoming feminine,
and feeling unlovable, unworthy, or not good enough. Love for men
can be complex and terrifying; therefore, it takes balls of courage
to really experience heartfelt love.

🔘 LEONARD

Growing up I never heard the words, "I love you." My parents were in survival mode, so affirming words were not part of their vocabulary. As a result, I felt awkward about saying or even hearing the words, "I love you." Many years ago, when I was studying family therapy, I attended a workshop that explored the impact of our childhood on our ability to love. The facilitator asked the participants to say aloud, "I love myself." At first, I choked on the words. I had a hard enough time speaking the words, let alone expressing them in a group. That workshop helped me wake up to my feeling of being unloved and forced me to grow into love.

🔘 RICK

Expressing love was difficult for me in my first marriage. In fact, it was so evident that my wife and I often joked that we were "young likers," instead of young lovers. That statement causes me pain even today. My then wife, a victim of terrible childhood sexual abuse, had a difficult time simply saying to me, "I love you." Instead, she'd say things like, "I appreciate you and the way you father our daughters." Or "You're a good man, Rick." But I yearned to hear those magic words from her and also yearned to say them freely to her. Strangely, both of us could say to our daughters, "I love you." Since we had such a hard time loving each other, it was no wonder that we eventually divorced.

If we experienced childhood neglect, abandonment, or abuse while growing up, it makes sense that we would have difficulty with love. We may yearn to have a loving relationship and feel loved; however, traumas of the past will impact our ability to build a life of love. Even if we were raised in a nurturing household, we would bear invisible scars from the past. As Harville Hendrix, creator of Imago Relationship Therapy, wrote, "… from the moment you were born you were a complex, dependent creature with a never-ending cycle of needs.... And no parents, no matter how devoted, are able to respond perfectly to all of those changing needs."[15]

Those wounds taught us about conditional love. In order to survive, we learned to act in certain ways to satisfy our needs and receive love from our caregivers. We then projected our early experiences of love onto the world. If one or both of our parents were emotionally unavailable or we felt smothered as children, we will anticipate the same unless we have an emotionally corrective experience of real love, which is unconditional.

The common version of love is the conditional model where we adapted to our environment by feeling, thinking, and behaving in ways that would bring us attention, acceptance, and love. If achieving brought accolades, then we worked hard on accomplishment. If pleasing others brought positive attention, we adopted that behavior. If manipulation or bullying made us feel more adequate or in control, then we utilized those behaviors to get what we wanted.

Men's socialization, which is quite different from women's, impacts our ability to grow into love. Nancy Chodorow highlights the differences when discussing attachment. As babies, both genders start life attached to their mother and experience love through her. "A girl, then, can develop a personal identification with her mother, because she has a real relationship with her that grows out of their early primary tie."[16] Boys, however, must developmentally detach from their mother to create an identity separate from her. This means that a boy "... tends to reject what he takes to be the feminine world."[17] As a result, masculinity stresses differentiation from others and the denial of emotions while femininity stresses a relational process that includes mutuality and emotions. When men reject

---

15   Hendrix, Harville, *Getting the Love You Want: A Guide for Couples*, Owl Books, New York, 1988, p. 15.

16   Chodorow, Nancy, *The Reproduction of Mothering: Psychoanalysis and the Sociology of Gender*, University of California Press, Berkeley, 1978, p. 175.

17   Ibid, p. 176.

what is perceived as the feminine world, true masculine love, when not modeled by emotionally unavailable fathers, is harder to access.

As a result, we are more likely to identify with the images of masculinity as portrayed in the media and by culture. Consider how the iconic figure James Bond is portrayed in movies when he falls in love. For him, like many action figures, love is driven by sexual attraction. The old adage often rings true that men turn to sex to feel connected and loved, whereas women want to feel connected and loved to have sex.

Action becomes a man's way of expressing love. This fits with the old model of masculinity that focuses on doing, rather than being in the world. If we are good enough, strong enough, smart enough, or success-ful enough, then we will be loved. Unfortunately, this outcome depends on external praise and reinforcement. We can be extremely success-ful in the outside world yet be miserable on the inside. Worthiness doesn't come from the outside; it comes from the inside—where real love exists. And we all long for real love and acceptance.

In *Real Love*, Greg Baer says, "Real Love is caring about the happiness of another person without any thought for what we might get for ourselves. When we give Real Love, we're not disappointed, hurt, or angry, even when people are thoughtless or inconsiderate or give us nothing in return—even gratitude—because our concern is for their happiness, not our own. Real Love is unconditional."[18]

To build a life of love, we must find that place within. That means we have to move past our defenses and cultural images of masculinity. If we grew up with guilt, shame, rejection, or abuse, we have likely erected barriers around our hearts and carried on stoically.

We access the power tool of love by living the words of the mystic Rumi: "Your task is not to seek for love, but merely to seek and find all the barriers within yourself that you have built against it." Building a life of love requires us to find the beliefs that act as

---

18   Baer, Greg, *Real Love: The Truth about Unconditional Love and Fulfilling Relationships*, Gotham Books, New York, 2003, p. 4.

barriers such as "I don't deserve love." "Love depends on the way I act or look." "If you see the real me, you won't love me."

After becoming aware of our unspoken and often unconscious beliefs, we need those balls of courage to face and dismantle the negative ones about love. However, that evolution requires us to welcome all facets of our lives, including the emotions and shadows we fear.

Becoming aware of our beliefs allows us to heal our wounded hearts. As Rumi also said, "The wound is the place where the light enters you." When the light of love enters us, we expand our heart and learn to truly love ourselves unconditionally. Without that self-love, we will love only upon the condition that we be loved.

So how do we practice self-love? *Brené Brown* wrote in *The Gifts of Imperfection*, "We cultivate love when we allow our most vulnerable and powerful selves to be deeply seen and known, and when we honor the spiritual connection that grows from that offering with trust, respect, kindness, and affection. Love is not something we give or get; it is something that we nurture and grow."[19]

As Jerry Jampolsky writes in *Love Is Letting Go of Fear*, "Love is the total absence of fear. Love asks no questions. Its natural state is one of extension and expansion, not comparison and measurement.[20]"

Since love is inherent in each of us, we don't have to find it. We are hard-wired for love and merely need to access it. Love is inherently our natural state of being and has nothing to do with performance, accomplishments, status, or any other cravings of the ego. It is unconditional, without guilt or shame and without boundaries or expectations. Love simply encompasses all of who we are.

---

19 Brown, Brené, *The Gifts of Imperfection: Let Go of Who You Think You're Supposed to Be and Embrace Who You Are*, Hazelden, Center City, MN, 2010, p. 26.

20 Jampolsky, Gerald, *Love Is Letting Go of Fear*, Celestial Arts, Berkeley, CA, 1979, p.17.

We can learn to love from the inside out by using these simple power tools:

1. Recognize who you are and where you've come from. Your ancestors and your history shaped your story to be what it is today.

2. Acknowledge your wounds and the defenses you built to survive outside attacks.

3. Forgive yourself for closing your heart to others, blaming others, and not being available to give or receive unconditional love. Forgiveness is the healing balm for any wounds.

4. Accept yourself the way you are. Even though you may be frightened of opening your heart, you can still accept that you are fearful of getting hurt, and still move forward.

5. Make a commitment to be more loving to yourself. This involves acts of self-care in thoughts and in deeds. The more you love yourself, the more love you will have for your neighbor.

6. Step into courage and open your heart to others. The word *courage* stems from the Latin word, *cor*, which means *heart*. With courage, you can love with an open heart and inspire others to expand their love.

As we open our heart, we step into the different shapes and sizes of love.

Fatherly love conveys protection, caring, strength, appreciation, joy, admiration, and tenderness. The flavor of fatherly love can be captured in the images of a father cradling an infant, comforting a two-year-old son or daughter, playing with his children, or teaching a child lessons or skills. That type of love nurtures a child's growth and development.

Imagine being a child on the receiving end of that love. He or she would feel safe and secure, appreciated and valued, comforted and cared for. Having received that type of love, the child could easily embrace a mentor, ask for help, feel a deep and profound love for self, and share that love with a brother or sister.

Brotherly love is about seeing other men and women as members of our family. We treat them with understanding and acceptance, compassion and forgiveness, tenderness and heartfelt joy. From that place we can extend love beyond an open heart and encourage, support, even challenge our brothers and sisters to create a loving world. We can love our neighbors as ourselves for we belong to the same family of man.

Romantic love expands our heart by taking us outside of ourselves into the inner sanctum of another where the power of two creates a powerful one—a union of hearts, minds, and spirits. While romantic love, or eros, awakens the senses, deepens feelings, and expands the heart to become a bigger vessel, it also activates an inner fire to transform and heal. Passionate love can be intoxicating and addictive. When we fall in love, we want to hold onto the intense feelings that we associate with a special partner. We often crave that special relationship to create the love chemicals in our brain. Partners may trigger chemical combustion, but the love factory is an inside job. Our inner state triggers the chemical reaction.

Dr. Daniel G. Amen's book, *The Brain in Love*, highlights attraction chemicals such as testosterone, estrogen, and pheromones; infatuation chemicals like serotonin, dopamine, and epinephrine; and bonding chemicals like oxytocin and vasopressin. These feel-good chemicals make us feel happy, alive, connected, and loved.

Who wouldn't want to feel that way? And if we stop producing those chemicals, it's no wonder we fall into despair.

Self-love summons us to become self-generating lovers so we can access the feeling of love, no matter what's going on outside of us. If our love tank is empty, we have little to give. Self-love nourishes and refuels. The more love we generate, the more love we can give. *Brené* Brown writes, "Practicing self-love means learning how to trust ourselves, to treat ourselves with respect, and to be kind and affectionate toward ourselves. This is a tall order given how hard most of us are on ourselves."[21]

We men are notoriously bad at self-care. As a result, we tend to look to our partners to care for us. Once we connect with our senses, bodies, and our feelings, we can notice our needs and desires, the first step to self-care, as *Brené* Brown says.

Once we master self-love, we can then love our partners more fully. Gary Chapman, a therapist who wrote *The 5 Love Languages: The Secret to Love That Lasts* identifies five ways that help us give and receive love: physical touch and affection, words of appreciation, quality time, acts of service, and gifts.[22] Each of us tends to prefer one or more of the languages that generate loving feelings, and we tend to use that language on others.

PHYSICAL TOUCH AND AFFECTION

Infants need touch. If they are not held, they fail to thrive. As we age, we have the same need for touch and affection. Children and grandchildren readily supply that need. Baths, showers, and massages stimulate our skin. Dogs and cats give us unconditional love. But we can ask for and share hugs which boost our physical and

---

21   Brown, Op. Cit., p. 27.

22   Chapman, Gary, *The Five Love Languages: The Secret to Love That Lasts*, Northfield Publishing, Chicago, IL, 2015.

emotional health. If we hug for six seconds or more, we release oxytocin, a bonding chemical that generates a feeling of belonging. The renowned therapist Virginia Satir famously said: "We need four hugs a day for survival, eight hugs a day for maintenance, and twelve hugs a day for growth."

RICK

My first love language is physical touch with words of encouragement as a close second. Though I'm a very sensual man, I was touch deprived for much of my adult life. No wonder I was in such dissonance in my first marriage. Looking back, it was amazing and sad to me that I lasted in my first marriage for twenty-three years with very little of either of my primary love languages fulfilled. Now that I am clear about my languages of love, I have established a deep, loving relationship with my current partner, Michele. Her love languages are identical to mine, so we both find it easy and natural to shower each other with loving affection. The awareness of our needs and the willingness and desire to satisfy them change everything!

LEONARD

As a child, I didn't receive much affection from my parents. My lack of physical contact created a longing for touch. Since I'm single and still need touch, I gravitate toward people who enjoy hugging. When I greet friends, family, or the men in the group, I welcome them with a loving bear hug. The physical contact establishes a sense of belonging and generates love.

I am also touched by the environment. When I lived in Chicago, I suffered from seasonal affective disorder which comes from the lack of sunshine, so living in a sunny, warm environment like California makes my body feel loved. So do massage and swimming.

WORDS OF APPRECIATION AND PRAISE

Cognitive Behavioral Therapy helps us reprogram negative beliefs with positive ones. Old wounds can be healed when we express positive affirmations to ourselves. Genuine words of praise help us love ourselves and others.

🫂 LEONARD

Since I rarely heard words of appreciation as a child, I tell them daily to myself and to others. At the end of every therapy session with clients, I acknowledge something positive about them such as their honesty, courage, or willingness to change.

I ask couples to share appreciations about themselves and their partner. Heartfelt words act as a powerful elixir to promote love.

I periodically tell my friends, "If no one has told you today that you're amazing (or some other affirming quality), let me be the first to tell you." The positive response that I receive is just as rewarding for me as it is for them to hear the affirmation.

🫂 RICK

Since I didn't receive much praise from my father and only conditional love from my mother, I need to be appreciated and loved regularly. One aspect of my relationship with Michele that I dearly love is our monthly check-ins that take place on the anniversary of our first date. We check in with what is working well in the relationship and how we can be better. We both look forward to this process as it gives us an opportunity to express our appreciation and love for each other. We also do a course correction, when necessary, to keep our relationship healthy and juicy. Michele's loving words become a healing balm to my soul. She gets to see the real me and reflects it in her feedback. Being seen and loved unconditionally, I have evolved my love for her beyond an open heart.

QUALITY TIME

This language of love sends the message that we're important and special. When we make time for friends, conversation, men's gatherings, walks in nature, exercise, meditation, or relaxing, we validate activities that increase our self-worth. Friends and lovers appreciate the special time, even a phone call or text, as it conveys care and attention.

RICK

I love riding my 2005 Harley Davidson Heritage Motorcycle with its cool custom paint and lots of chrome. People tend to think of bikers as tough guys not to mess with. I must say that I do enjoy the projections that are placed on me as I roar up the road.

The roar of the engine and the flash of sunlight off the shiny parts of my blue bike exhilarate me. I simply love the quality time—whether alone or in groups of other men. While riding, I clear my head, check in with my senses, and feel totally alive! It's the perfect antidote to my pattern of shutting down, isolating, and ignoring the messages of my body and soul because I must pay attention to what's around me at all times to be safe. I can't check out with the wind in my face and the sun on my body.

I moved to Southern California in large part to ride year-round. That's a lot of quality time, whether it's a short hop to the grocery store or a week-long ride and camping trip to a National Park like Zion or Arches.

My favorite rides occur with some buddies from my men's group who regularly take our bikes into the foothills of the coastal mountains or along the beach. We check in with our lives at our frequent stops for gas, food, beverages, and bio breaks. (These stops occur more frequently as we age!) The immense joy and gratitude are so intense that I can almost feel my heart leaping through my leather jacket!

🐾 LEONARD

When I was a boy and my mother found me reading a book, she would say, "Don't just sit there. Do something!" As a single parent, she always found work for me to do. As an adult, I made an agreement with myself not to work on Sundays. That day would be reserved to DO NOTHING! Just writing those words generates self-care because I can drive myself mercilessly to accomplish and achieve. My doing nothing rule means that I do nothing on Sunday that feels like work. That means visiting a local resort overlooking the beach and sipping a coffee and reading a good book. Doing nothing may prompt me to connect with friends over a meal, attend a church service, take a luxurious nap, swim at the gym, or attend a personal growth workshop.

The quality time of doing nothing at the end of the week rejuvenates me with self-care so that when Monday rolls around, I'm ready to hop on my metaphorical motorcycle and burn rubber with love.

ACTS OF SERVICE

Men typically show their love through acts of service like fixing problems or doing things for our partner. Women often complain about their male partners who don't listen to them but instead leap into fixing them or the problem. What they often don't realize is that fixing makes us feel important and successful. We can practice acts of self-care by fixing an unhealthy eating problem, staying in shape, or washing our car. We can also volunteer our services to help others.

🐾 LEONARD

During one of my walks by the beach, I encountered a boy who was trying to untangle his fishing line. I used to fish a lot with my son so I asked if he wanted some help. He gratefully accepted my assistance to unravel his fishing line. By the time his line was straightened out, both he and I were happy. I was able to share my care and he could resume his fishing.

Some of the acts of service I give to myself to feel loved include organizing a massage, cooking a favorite meal like zucchini lasagna, and walking by the beach.

RICK

Michele loves it when I fix something broken in her house, especially her electronics. She says, "It's a real turn-on when you put on your tool belt, Rick, and fix something that's not working. I love watching you figure out what needs to be done and then do it." I receive great joy out of offering these simple acts of service which cements our relationship in a win-win way.

GIFTS

Stereotypically, women like flowers, chocolates, or clothes, while guys have enjoyed computer gadgets, tools, fishing gear, or cars. (Notice that women's gifts are relatively inexpensive, while men's are not!) Giving presents lets someone know that we are thinking about them, and when we receive a present, we can experience the joy of being loved. Gifts do not have to be material. A person's presence can often be their present.

RICK

One of the best gifts I ever received was an overstuffed recliner I got for Father's Day some years ago. I still feel warm and loved when I sit in that chair. It brings back fond memories of sitting there with my daughters snuggling in my lap while we watched TV or read the Sunday funnies together.

LEONARD

When I was a boy, I loved to visit my Polish grandmother who was called Busha. Living in the apartment below my family, she would serve me toast and hot coffee with sweetened condensed milk for breakfast. Yum!

That loving memory gets recreated every time I treat myself to a creamy latte.

Since my daughter and her family live in Australia, I gift myself a trip there every year. I bring a suitcase of gifts for my grandchildren. I have just as much fun buying them as watching them open the presents.

As we build a life of love, we become self-generating lovers and keep the brain's chemical factory in high production of love drugs. However, we are ultimately called to share that love with the world. We call this loving beyond an open heart. This becomes easier when we hang out with other men and women who are also committed to spreading love in the world.

A global awareness is shifting our consciousness from the separateness of "I" to a "We" interconnectedness. This We-Space transcends our individuality so that we become more than a collection of separate hearts. We-Space creates a collective open-heart. Where two or more are gathered in the name of love, magic happens. Every relationship becomes a holy encounter.

Patricia Albere, one of the pioneers in this movement, wrote, "People are starting to awaken together, both in paired relationships and in community collectives.... Today, Evolutionary Relationships represent the unfolding edge of our development as a human species. In truth, the longing is not our desire for divine love so much as divine love desiring and needing us. This new dimension of love and more evolved consciousness needs our surrender and our wholehearted cooperation."[23]

23 Albere, Op. Cit., pp 5-6.

Albere wrote a wonderful blog where she described the NBA world champion Golden State Warriors as a team that represents "…a new paradigm that is the next evolutionary wave of consciousness. It goes beyond the personal and the individual, and stretches us into a space of a living, dynamic and powerful unitive awareness that can only come into being when we engage it *together*."[24] She highlights five ways the Warriors demonstrate this paradigm: They embrace the collective over personal glory, adopt a sharing style of play, play as one organism, improvise and adapt with an evolutionary attitude, and play for the joy of the game.

Imagine loving from that We-Space. Like the Golden State Warriors, we can put aside our egos and bring the dimension of love to our relationships. Rather than viewing differences as separating us, we can appreciate each player as contributing an integral element of the team. No doubt, we will stumble and lose some games along the way, but if we continue to use our power tools of love, we become part of a team of men dedicated to creating a world of love and peace.

Connected with one heart, we can now build a life with **Authenticity**, the next tool in the CLASSICS brand of power tools.

---

24 Albere, Patricia, "5 Ways the Collective Consciousness of the Warriors Is Reshaping the Future of the NBA (and Beyond)," July 21, 2017.

STRETCH INTO LOVE

1. What barriers have you built that prevent you from giving love? From receiving love?

2. What's at risk if you let down your defenses?

3. How can you open your heart to love?

4. What is your language of love? (Touch, Words of Appreciation, Quality Time, Acts of Service, or Gifts)

5. Consider instituting a daily practice of self-care and love. What can you do?

6. How can you share that love with a loved one? With other men? The world?

Chapter Five

Build a Life of Authenticity

We can only belong when we offer our most authentic selves and when we're embraced for who we are.

— Brené Brown

O nce upon a time a young lad named Reginald lived in a castle with his adoring parents. His father, a knight held in high esteem in the king's court, proudly displayed the shining silver armor to his son before he mounted his stallion and rode off to battle invaders, kill dragons, or rescue damsels in distress. Reginald so admired his father that he imagined being just like him.

As he grew up, his father taught the importance of protective armor, and on his son's thirteenth birthday presented him with the first suit of polished metal. Reginald was so enamored with his armor that he wore it whenever he played with other boys. In time, he joined his father in the king's court as Sir Reginald. He battled invaders, defeated dragons, and even rescued a damsel in distress who eventually became his wife.

When Sir Reginald had a son, he started instructing him about being a knight, just as his father had taught him. However, since he spent considerable time riding his steed, whenever he returned to the castle, he kept his metal suit on so that he could always be prepared for battle.

This did not bode well with his wife. She complained that his armor stopped her from getting through to him. Sir Reginald defended himself, saying that a knight's job was to protect the castle. He did acknowledge, however, that armor prevented him from getting close to his wife, his son, and even the other knights who wore armor.

When his wife told him that she could no longer live with a man who was cold and stiff, Sir Reginald chose to remove the armor. Not surprisingly, he had a hard time taking it off. He had worn it for so long, he had forgotten how to live without it. As a result, he was so well defended that he had lost the ability to feel. Desperate to keep his wife and reclaim his feelings, he made the courageous decision to take a course on Armor Removal.

Like Sir Reginald, we carry heavy armor of protection from days long past whether we know it or not. Even when no one is attacking us, we unconsciously armor ourselves for defense.

In his book, Knights Without Armor, Aaron Kipnis, PhD, states, "In America today there appears to be an attitude that boys do not need or deserve the same degree of nurturance, safety, intimacy, love, and support to which girls are entitled. Boys are weaned earlier than girls and thus deprived of natural tranquilizers and the immune system support of mother's milk—not to mention the soothing comfort of the breast. Coincidentally, boys tend to lag about four to six weeks behind girls in their development. They crawl, sit, and speak later and tend to cry more during infancy."[25]

---

25 Kipnis, Aaron, *Knights Without Armor*, Jeremy P. Tarcher, Los Angeles, CA. 1991, pp 21.

Kipnis states that as men develop, "…we are encouraged to repress pain. This attitude is continually reinforced during our adult lives. If we cry out in pain, we'll be labeled sissy, wimp, or whiner and risk being shamed for appearing unmasculine."[26] He goes on to say, "This conditioning betrays our innate sensitivity as children. It is not surprising, therefore, to note that young boys are admitted to mental hospitals and juvenile institutions about seven times more frequently than girls of similar age and socioeconomic background."[27]

Kipnis asks us to work together to drop our armor, act in integrity, and become more authentic and accountable. Easily said but much harder for many of us men to do. Having low integrity and not being accountable are byproducts of being conditioned as a male. If we cannot trust our senses and we are shamed for having feelings, how can we ever become fully expressed, integrated, and accountable? When our words and actions don't match how we feel, we know we are incongruent. When men are asked to describe what it feels like to be incongruent, they often say, "It feels bad. Like I'm a liar or hiding my truth."

LEONARD

After my father left the family, I developed a severe case of eczema on my hands and arms. At ten years of age, I hated my ugly rash. My mother had been trained as a nurse and applied creams and ointments, but they didn't help. When they became infected, I tried to keep the red sores hidden. I didn't want to tell my mother who was on overload as she struggled to make ends meet as a single parent raising four children. When overwhelmed, my mother would vent her frustration in anger. Rather than facing her wrath for having

26 Ibid., pp 22

27 Ibid., p. 23.

infected skin, I tried treating the sores with peroxide, hoping they would go away. Only when the infection spread, did I reach out for help. Thankfully, she replied sympathetically instead of launching into shaming me for causing the problem.

I didn't realize it back then, but my suit of armor had already been installed to protect myself from being attacked, blamed, or shamed. Yet my inner anguish was revealed to the outside world in an angry rash, indicating lots of emotions festering on the inside. Behind that armor, I felt alone and isolated and went through my childhood keeping many of my feelings and needs hidden. When I started studying psychology, I realized how the heavy defensive armor not only stopped me from talking about my inner pain and revealing myself to others, but it also sapped my energy.

Brené Brown, who wrote the book *The Gifts of Imperfection: Let Go of Who You Think You're Supposed to Be and Embrace Who You Are*, said that incongruent living is exhausting. It's hard to connect with feelings and share our love when we protect ourselves with heavy armor. So many of us men try to live incongruently, angry that the people we care about can't break through our defenses, yet we desperately cling to our armor's seeming protection.

RICK

The tears streamed down my little sister's face as our mom finished spanking her. She was only two years old, but that did not spare her from the rage-full wrath of our schizophrenic mother. She was the fourth child in the row to suffer this treatment. We were all crying loudly and uncontrollably now, as we stood in line awaiting more beatings.

For round two, mom moved to me, the oldest child at nine years old. Determined to get a confession from one of us, she screamed again, "Who left the dirty sock on the floor?"

None of us answered. We were locked in terror as she went to work on me. I hadn't done the deed that had set her off, but I knew the beatings would continue until someone confessed. I could see it in her eyes.

A loving, protective part in me suddenly came to life. As the oldest sibling, I was the one responsible for stopping this. In that instant, I decided that I would end this carnage by confessing, knowing full well that this would only bring more punishment my way. At least the pain would be over for my siblings.

My mother stopped. She looked at me with angry eyes and spat out, "Ricky, your lying has led to this. You owe your brothers and sister for putting them through this. You will apologize to each of them now and do their chores for the next week by yourself."

I said nothing. I meekly and tearfully turned to apologize to my sibs. Even though I was hurting on the outside, deep inside, I felt good to have acted to stop this insanity and spare my sibs more pain. Thus, at the age of nine, I took on the role of a knight in shining armor. That armor stopped something horrible from occurring, but it also cost me access to my true self.

We encourage men to access their true self by connecting with senses, feelings, and relationships while also living with a loving heart. These create a loving space to crack open and be our authentic selves. The process of building an authentic life asks us to drill beneath the concrete slabs of beliefs that we were taught as children, face our shadows, and discover the gold underneath.

Authenticity pulls us deep within to discover our truths. It requires us to recognize the physical sensations, feelings, and thoughts that we are experiencing and then express them clearly and directly with maturity. Authenticity then becomes something we *are*, not something we simply *do*.

Authenticity involves truth, honesty, realness, vulnerability, reliability, and genuineness. It requires self-awareness and self-disclosure. We cannot speak our truth if we do not actually know, feel, and acknowledge it.

In the classic children's book, *The Velveteen Rabbit* by Maggie Williams Bianco, the Skin Horse teaches the Velveteen Rabbit about becoming real. He says, "It doesn't happen all at once. You become. It takes a long time. That's why it doesn't often happen to people who break easily, or have sharp edges, or who must be carefully kept. Generally, by the time you are Real, most of your hair has been loved off, and your eyes drop out and you get loose in the joints and very shabby. But these things don't matter at all, because once you are Real you can't be ugly, except to people who don't understand."[28]

During the course of our lives, we, Rick and Leonard, continually work at "being real." We have experienced the cost of bearing heavy armor. Peeling off that armor involves the risk of revealing our authentic, emotional selves. Doing so doesn't mean that we don't get hit with arrows from those who don't understand and prefer the armored way. We know that the practice of authenticity takes time and a commitment to move past the outer layers of limiting beliefs. Staying aligned with telling the truth about our feelings, thoughts, and deeds is not an easy skill to master because we, like other men, have been taught from early on to hide our true feelings, not acknowledge our shortcomings or our problems, and act tough and confident even when we are not. In other words, to be inherently inauthentic from the get-go.

We can build an authentic life of integrity and accountability by using these six tools:

1. Notice your armor.

2. Find a safe place to peel off the armor.

28
Williams Bianco, Maggie, *The Velveteen Rabbit,* Random House, New York, NY, 1922, p. 17.

3. Mine your shadows.

4. Welcome feedback.

5. Stay in integrity.

6. Be accountable.

1. NOTICE YOUR ARMOR.

Most of us have become so attached to our armor that we identify with it, believing that is who we are. We may shut off our senses and feelings and defend our behavior even if it causes others pain. We walk in the world, clinking and clanking, in armor that others can see but we cannot. Unfortunately, pain is one of the prime motivators that forces us to pay attention. Pain in our body, relationships, and workplace will highlight our armor—if we are willing to go there.

When the pain of living is greater than the pain of change, we become receptive to change. We are more willing to look at ourselves and our behavior and even attend counseling, twelve-step programs, or an intensive men's personal growth weekend. Those avenues offer a mirror where we can face ourselves and our armored identity.

Self-awareness coupled with a non-judgmental manner brings our attention to those places where we feel stuck. We may notice tense shoulders, feelings of loneliness, or a preoccupation with recurring thoughts. We can ask ourselves where we are shut down and disconnected from our feelings. We can notice when we relate to others in a defensive way or inhibit ourselves from speaking our truth. We can also discover when and how we engage in conflict or avoid it. We can also uncover shadows, those repressed parts of ourselves that we cannot see. Once we are willing to notice our armor, we can peel it off. But first we need a safe place.

2. FIND A SAFE PLACE TO PEEL OFF THE ARMOR.

Armor worked well for a man—as long as he was on his horse. However, when a knight fell off his steed, he became virtually helpless on the ground. This is a metaphor for modern man. He may not even know that he's fallen until he realizes how helpless he is locked inside heavy armor.

Men's groups offer a place where a fallen knight can let down his guard and get help. We often talk about creating safe containers in which to do our work. In essence, that means being in a safe, caring place where we feel accepted and where confidentiality will be honored. The important key is safety. We are not going to take off our armor if under attack. That safe place may be in therapy, self-help groups, or personal growth programs. We can then take the next step of authenticity by learning about our unconscious parts.

Safe containers where we can practice living without armor are rare in families, relationships, or organizations. We are both extremely grateful for our men's group where we can show up and identify where we are stuck, receive feedback, and take steps to change. By doing so, we peel away the armor and get real with one another.

RICK

A number of years ago, I attended a retreat with Robert Bly, a well-known poet and leader of the mythopoetic arm of the Men's Movement. At that retreat, pieces of red ribbon were passed out to each man in the group with instructions to tie a ribbon on any part of our body where we suffered wounds, scars, or broken bones.

There was silence as we thoughtfully and thoroughly completed the assigned task. Many of us repeatedly went back to the pile of red ribbons in the center of our circle to get more. I, myself, lost track of how many ribbons I had tied onto my body.

After about fifteen minutes, we were then instructed to tie ribbons where we had emotional, sexual, spiritual, or psychic wounds. The room got quieter as we faced our invisible scars of shame. Some softly sobbed while others wore grim looks on their faces as memories of ancient pain surfaced.

After the last man tied the last ribbon on his body, we formed a circle. We stood in silence for a while, staring at the stunning sight before us: a sea of red. Our bodies were covered from head to toe with dozens of ribbons—from our cocks, down to our legs, up to our heads and everywhere in between.

After a few moments, some of us began to wail as we witnessed our own and our brothers' pain. Soon, the entire circle was grieving our collective wounds—both outer and inner. We held each other as we allowed ourselves to feel, to really feel, the pain we held from the deep wounding that the "Man Box" had set us all up for.

After a time, the wailing ceased, and we took a seat on the floor. In turn, we each spoke of our wounds, pointing out when and where we had received this physical wound, that emotional stabbing, this shame, and that spiritual slight. Some of us cried when others spoke. Others remarked that they had never spoken of the incidents that they shared. A few became angry and one man simply could not speak.

As we identified our pain, we untied our ribbons and returned them to the growing pile in the center of the circle. When we were complete, we felt incredibly bonded and connected.

I'll never forget that ceremony nor the brothers who shared it with me. At the end of the evening, I thought to myself, "Our armor doesn't really protect us; it simply hides our pain behind shiny metal."

3. MINE YOUR SHADOWS.

The concept of a *Shadow* comes from the teaching of Carl Jung, the famous nineteenth-century Swiss psychiatrist and contemporary of Freud. In Jungian terms, a shadow is the part of us we hide, repress, or deny. The shadow can be both dark and gold. If we shine a light in front of our body, our actual shadow falls behind us, and we can't see it. Jung said that what we repress and are unaware of leaks out unconsciously in sideways behaviors that hurt ourselves and others. In the process, we deny valuable parts of ourselves. When this phenomenon happens in our lives, we rob ourselves of vitality and lower our self-esteem.

All of us have wounded parts of ourselves that have been stored in the unconscious or dark shadow. Having done so, we lost access to that energy, feeling, or belief. For example, many of us were told as young boys by parents, teachers, and ministers that sex is dirty, wrong, and dangerous, even sinful, and that sex outside of marriage is wrong. If in childhood we were caught by our parents exploring our sexuality in innocent ways, often we were shamed. If we experienced sexual abuse, we carried that deeply etched shame forever in our minds. Negative or painful messages about sex, repeated many times, would cause us to repress aspects of our sexuality and block that vital energy.

If we never healed an aspect of our sexuality, we might act out sexually later in life and become an abuser or possibly use men or women in demeaning ways for gratification. Alternately, we might do the opposite and become passive sexually or even asexual as a defense. Both responses rob us of our vitality, for it takes a lot of energy to repress something as important to our existence as sex. (We will explore this more fully in Chapter Seven on sexuality.) Whenever we believe we are bad or wrong, defective and unworthy, or unimportant or unsuccessful, we will have a psychic cave filled with shadows.

Our shadows of gold represent the talents, gifts, lessons, self-love, and appreciation that define where we have come from and who we are. But while growing up, if we had heard harsh, negative, and critical words—such as we're not good enough, worthy enough, or loveable and then suppress those—we will hide our brilliance, beauty, talents, gifts, and competence. Thus, we create our golden shadow.

Many of our suppressed feelings, like fear, anger, shame, or sadness, fall into the shadow because they are considered unacceptable by society. As we mentioned before, common messages in American society are "Men don't cry" and "Only sissies are afraid." As men, we are allowed to express some of our anger, particularly in the arena of sports, but not our sadness, fear, or shame. As a result, we release many of our emotions through anger, often in a sideways manner. We express our fear as anger, our grief angrily, and even our joy as anger. (Men whack each other or chest bump when sharing joy during sporting events!) Sadly, many of us cannot find our authentic joy.

When we push emotions into shadows, we lose access to a range of feelings that enliven us and make us preciously human. At the same time, those blocked emotions look for a way out, to come into the light. If we are unconscious, they appear in dark, foreboding ways, hurting those around us.

Many of our behaviors may operate out of shadow—those secret actions we do when no one else is watching, like cheating on our taxes, having an affair, withholding love from a partner, or surfing the internet for personal purposes during work hours. According to Jung, these shadow behaviors drain our aliveness, create guilt and shame, and stifle our passion. Secrets also disconnect us from loved ones, friends, and coworkers.

When **dark** shadow behaviors occur and go unnoticed or unchallenged, dysfunctional relationships emerge. Careers become stymied, communication devolves into blame games, and marriages deteriorate. When our **golden** shadows are hidden, we become grandiose, narcissistic, ungrounded, or we denigrate or judge our own beauty and that of others. Notice here that *both* our darker parts *and* our golden parts can be in shadow. In fact, Marianne Williamson states in *A Return to Love*:

We ask ourselves, who am I to be brilliant, gorgeous, talented, fabulous? Actually, who are you not to be?... Our deepest fear is not that we are inadequate.

Our deepest fear is that we are powerful beyond measure.

It is our light, not our darkness, that most frightens us.[29]

We may be afraid of shining brightly. Others may be jealous or critical of who we simply are. As a result, our golden talents and attributes may be more deeply hidden in shadow than our darkness. Strangely, some of us are more comfortable talking about our dark qualities and the bad things we have done than about the beautiful golden qualities we have. This tendency is sadly common—especially among men.

We reclaim our authentic, healthy masculinity by illuminating our shadows. Kevin Cashman, in his book *Leadership from the Inside Out: Becoming a Leader for Life*, offers seven clues that shadows may be operating in our lives. We've summarized them below:

1. People give us feedback inconsistent with how we see ourselves.

2. We feel stuck or blocked with a real loss as to what to do next.

3. Our strengths become counterproductive.

4. We are not open to information, new learning, or other people's views.

5. We react to circumstances with emotional responses disproportionate to the situation.

29 Williamson, Marianne, *A Return to Love*, Foundation for Inner Peace, Harper Collins, New York, NY, 1992, pp. 165.

6. We find ourselves forcefully reacting to the limitations of others in a critical, judgmental way and projecting our shadow onto them.

7. We experience pain, trauma, or discomfort in our body.[30]

Any of these can indicate that a shadow is present and seeks the light. Cashman tells us, "Listen closely to your body as you uncover shadow beliefs." Wise words, indeed!

The more shadows we reclaim, the more parts of ourselves we can access, freeing us to be powerful leaders, fathers, partners, and friends. So how do we face our shadows? We use a process we call **Shadow Mining**.

To mine our shadows, we need to pay attention to how our behaviors affect others. If we continually impact others in ways that are different from what we intended, an *unintended impact*, then very likely, our shadow is "leaking out" on them. If we suppress our anger or sadness, the emotions will emerge elsewhere. For example, if we tell a partner that we love them yet treat them badly or have an affair, hidden feelings likely reside in shadow. If our partner reacts to that betrayal out of his/her own shadow, the relationship gets ugly and painful. If we say something sarcastic to a friend, our shadow may be acting out, especially if we excuse it by saying, "I was only joking. What's your problem?" If we notice a beautiful or wonderful behavior in a family member and withhold our sharing or praise, then we may also be acting out of shadow. Shadows are insidious and require constant inspection and awareness to ferret them out and heal. Shadow mining becomes a life-long commitment to finding our true self.

We can also mine our shadows by watching who we project them on. (See Cashman's clue #6.) We project our shadows, both the dark and the gold, onto other people as if they are a projection screen. The projected dark shadows show up when we harshly

---

30 Cashman, Kevin, *Leadership from the Inside Out: Becoming a Leader for Life*, Berrett-Koehler Publishers, 2017, p. 43.

judge others for the very behaviors we do when no one is looking. The harsher our judgment, the deeper our shadows. If we always notice angry people, we're probably holding onto anger.

Consider the people you judge, hate, or despise. What qualities do they have that you dislike? Now look inside yourself and notice whether you have any of those qualities. You may hate dishonesty but see areas in your life where you sometimes lie.

Likewise, someone we admire or hold in high esteem can represent a positive or golden quality that we have in shadow. "If you spot it, you got it!" is a well-known psychological truism. Others often mirror those parts that we hide, suppress, or deny.

LEONARD

My Chicago men's group went on a retreat together. During one exercise, we looked around the room and made a list of all the positive qualities we liked about each other. Next, we repeated the process and listed all the negative qualities that we spotted. That was the harder exercise for me as I had to consciously look at each man and notice what I did not like. After we had written both lists, a large mirror was placed in front of a chair. Each man took a turn sitting on that hot seat and looking into the mirror. Then we reviewed each negative quality and made an "I" statement based on the list, such as "I am arrogant, I am anxious, I am insecure, etc." Then we moved to the positive qualities and repeated "I" statements for each of them. "I am brilliant, I am compassionate, I am loving, etc." Though the process was difficult at times, the safety of the group made it easier to own my darker shadows and my gold.

As you mine your shadow, you can reclaim those sacred and powerful parts of your soul that have been ignored or denied. You can also take action to alter your behaviors.

4. WELCOME FEEDBACK.

We often have a hard time seeing our shadows; however, others do not. Usually, a partner is the first to notice them. We can mine our shadows by soliciting those we trust for feedback and really listen to them. Asking for and receiving honest feedback take courage. We can offer clear, clean feedback when asked. Doing so even helps us grow and evolve. How else can we build authentic relationships if both parties are defending themselves with armor? Feedback helps us see what we cannot see. Others simulate a mirror so that we can see other sides of ourselves and take steps to grow and evolve.

One simple rule when taking feedback: if we have an emotional or physical signal of truth like an immediate repulsion, a smile, or tears, then that feedback is worth exploring as a part of our shadow. If feedback does not fit, then we can simply let it go.

LEONARD

I participate in several groups that provide continual feedback. I enjoy my Toastmasters meetings because after each speech, an evaluator offers constructive criticism on what worked and what didn't. Over the years that feedback has helped me develop the craft of presenting talks.

I have participated in many writing critique groups over the past thirty-five years. One of the guidelines in such groups is that the author remains quiet while receiving feedback. As a writer, I can accept or reject the feedback, but if I spend time debating with those giving feedback, I miss out on their helpful comments and advice.

RICK

My ex-wife noticed that I appeared to be angry while, at the same time, I smiled. This behavior was not only incongruent but confused those in my life who were unsure whether to respond to my anger or my smile. Bringing this to my attention has allowed me to become conscious of when I did this and allowed me to alter this behavior so that I could act congruently.

When we fastidiously practice giving and receiving honest, authentic feedback, we become trustworthy. We encounter enough bullshit in life. To be with men who don't bullshit but speak the truth strengthens our resolve to live with integrity.

5. STAY IN INTEGRITY.

Integrity is used to connote a person who fulfills his or her commitments and lives by a clear moral code. The word also describes a person who is whole, meaning that he continually becomes aware of the many aspects of his personality and integrates them so that his thoughts, words, actions, and feelings are congruent and in alignment with what he says. A man of integrity says what he means directly and honestly.

The world is hungry for leaders with integrity. "Alternate facts," lying, blaming, finger-pointing, and disowning responsibility are behaviors that represent the antithesis to living a life of integrity. Men who live in integrity are enlivened, caring, and engaged. They own up to their mistakes and offer amends to right them.

We activate our integrity by identifying our moral code and what is important to us. In Japan, this is called *bushido*. We live in accordance with that code, no matter how hard. We can enlist the support of people who are willing—and many will help if asked— to bring our shadows to the light.

If we appear to be incongruent with our words, emotions, or deeds, we can invite others to bring that to our attention. We can then recognize the parts of us that hide and bring them into the light.

6. BE ACCOUNTABLE.

Accountability is different from integrity in that it asks us to be responsible for our actions and their impact on others, no matter what our intentions. We don't get a pass on our behaviors and their effects on people just because we didn't mean to cause a problem or pain. Instead of blaming others for reacting badly to our words or behaviors or accusing them of overreacting, we can become aware of the way we are communicating and even change how we are relating.

Hiding our unattractive or unacceptable behaviors only lessens us as men, for we expend our energy in hiding and denying those behaviors and trying to appear perfect. Hiding depletes our passion and authentic manhood and, paradoxically, makes us untrustworthy, unattractive, and phony. Due to our early conditioning, putting on our armor becomes a default setting that we can easily slip into, especially when we are fatigued, impatient, or living our life unconsciously.

An accountable man owns the impacts of his behaviors, no matter the intention. We become aware of our *intent* versus *impact*. When we speak, we may have an intent. However, the impact shows us how our behaviors have landed on others. If our words or actions impact others differently from our intent, we can take corrective action. To be accountable, we must be willing to hear and see the impact of our behaviors and words, without blame or shame.

We use a five-step process of accountability that was developed in the ManKind Project. Whenever a man is out of accountability with himself or another, he is asked to answer these questions:

ACCOUNTABILITY IN FIVE SIMPLE STEPS

1. What is the behavior or broken agreement that impacted you or others?

91

2. What is the impact of that behavior on yourself? On others?

3. What belief about yourself (shadow) are you hiding or denying that appears in your behaviors or words?

4. Do you really want to change that behavior?

5. What Act of Accountability (AOA) are you willing to offer the other person(s) that will rebuild the interpersonal bridge? The AOA will remind you of any tendency to slip into hurtful unconscious behaviors or language.

We use the accountability process when we do not follow through with an agreement or when our behaviors or words negatively impact others, often experienced as an *ouch*. If others have the courage to speak up, they can help us take responsibility for our behavior and move back into accountability. Here's an example of working with this process.

On a men's weekend led by Rick, John stood up before the seventy men present and owned that he had not been accountable to his wife. He had been having an affair for six months with his secretary and was hiding it from his wife. [Step 1 – taking responsibility for not being accountable to his marriage vows.]

John saw the impact of his behaviors on his wife as he withheld affection and stopped being authentic with her. As well, he saw how he had set up his secretary to believe that he would eventually leave his wife and marry her, contributing to her guilt about breaking up a marriage. He recognized the price of the affair. John felt sadness and deep shame about hiding his behavior and guilt over what might happen if he were found out. [Step 2 – identifying the impact of his behavior on himself and others.]

He needed help to find the shadows behind his behavior [Step 3]. After a while, he identified the bottom-line shadow beliefs. Part of him wanted to blame his wife for his actions. Feedback from

Rick and other men showed him that *he* was responsible for his actions and that *his* behavior had created this situation. He eventually realized that he did not feel worthy of his wife's love. He also discovered feelings of being abandoned by her when their son was born, as she had put much of her love and energy into caring for their new child and less of him.

Saddened about losing the intimacy with his wife, John dropped his armor and cried. The cries turned into sobs as the room of seventy men silently and respectfully witnessed his profound despair. Clearly, he still loved his wife and wanted to salvage the relationship. With the support from the other men, John owned the previously unexpressed abandonment and the grief about his lifelong sense that he felt unworthy of love and even sabotaged it when he had it. As John authentically voiced these shadows that were unconsciously driving his behaviors, he straightened up.

Rick asked him, "Are you willing to change these behaviors?"

He answered, "You bet." [Step 4 – stating a commitment to change.]

"So what act of accountability would start the process of repairing your marriage?"

John became animated as he stated firmly, "I am ending my affair."

"When?"

"Immediately. My AOA is to go home Sunday and have an honest conversation with my wife about how much I love her. I'm going to tell her how I feel about our relationship and what I need from her and want for us. I will also ask her what she needs and wants. I am going to suggest that we get marriage counseling if she's willing." [Step 5 – stating the Act of Accountability.]

Tears streamed down John's cheeks as he talked about repairing his relationship with his wife. When asked how he thought his wife would respond to his request to have an honest conversation and work on their relationship, he answered, "I really hope she says yes. She knows things aren't good between us."

Rick asked John, "How do you feel now?"

He looked inside for a moment and, as surprise washed over his face, he stated, "I feel more joyful and hopeful about my marriage for the first time in a long time. I feel more alive and ready to do my work."

The men in the room spontaneously applauded John who stood tall without any armor.

The epilogue to this story is that John brought his wife to the Homecoming/Graduation exercise four days after his men's weekend. There were perhaps 150 people in the room, all celebrating and honoring those who had completed the training. During the graduation, friends and loved ones were asked to speak about the men in their lives who came home.

The first person to speak was John's wife. "My name is Jane. John and I have been married ten years. I don't know what you did to my husband last weekend, but the man who came home was a different man. He opened up and listened to me. We had the most honest conversation about our marriage we ever had. He became very emotional and took responsibility for screwing up. He fessed up to what he had done. I wanted to kill him. But he didn't defend himself or blame me like he had done in the past. That made me realize that maybe there was hope. We've had many talks over the past several days. I know he loves me and wants to improve the marriage. We have a way to go but plan to get counseling. I have real hope that our marriage can grow. After the weekend, John became the man I always wanted in my life. I can't thank you enough!"

Her heartfelt story touched everyone. Not a dry eye in the house. She took a deep breath and continued shyly, "And I want to share that we are having the best sex we've had in years!"

Rick has kept track of John and Jane and, to this day, their marriage has prospered. Obviously, their sex life had improved because they later added a daughter to the family. John's story is just one of hundreds of similar stories we have witnessed that attest to the power of authentically peeling off our armor, standing in integrity and accountability, and reclaiming our passion and truth as men!

If you don't have a men's group or twelve-step group to help you stay accountable, we suggest an accountability buddy. He or she can help you stay focused on keeping your agreements with yourself and others. Some men use accountability buddies to lose weight, quit smoking, practice self-care, eat healthy, and stay connected to relationships.

Accountability helps us maintain our integrity. Together, they create a foundation for us to stay committed to our evolution. If we fall back behind the protective armor when we really want to connect with an open heart, we can remember to notice our armor, find a safe place to peel off the armor, mine our shadows, welcome feedback, stay in integrity, and be accountable.

Now that we have covered Connection, Love, and Authenticity in the CLASSICS Model, we are ready to embrace our **Spirituality**.

AUTHENTICALLY STRETCH ACCOUNTABILITY AND INTEGRITY

1. How do you armor yourself? Are you aware of when you are wearing your armor? How does it stop you from being authentic?

2. What do you suppress or deny in yourself that would be considered dark shadows? How do they impact your life?

3. What great qualities or golden shadows do you suppress or deny? How can you reclaim those parts of yourself?

4. Who can you rely on for feedback about your behavior? How can you enlist their aid in helping you uncover your shadows?

5. What is your moral code or that which is important to you? How can you remain in integrity?

6. In what areas of your life are you accountable, or not accountable to yourself and others?

7. How does being accountable and not being accountable impact your relationships with yourself and others?

8. How could you perform an Act of Accountability to help you become more accountable?

9. Who can you enlist as an accountability buddy to keep you accountable?

Chapter Six

Build a Spiritual Life

The essential lesson I've learned in life is to just be yourself. Treasure the magnificent being that you are and recognize first and foremost you're not here as a human being only. You're a spiritual being having a human experience.

— Wayne Dyer

Inside a maximum-security prison, Rick joined twenty other men to help facilitate a men's circle to support the healing and growth of those who many believed should be "thrown away." Byron, a six-foot-tall, forty-eight-year-old African American inmate who was serving time for murder, stood before Rick, surrounded by other inmates and staffers. He was pissed off, not unusual for prisoners.

Rick asked Byron, "Who are you angry at?"

"I'm fucking pissed off at my dad and mom. Neither of them was there for me. Dad was a mean drunk and Mom used drugs when she wasn't working a job. They forced me to steal food and money for the family before I was five. I hate them. I fucking hate them for beating me! Never had a chance."

We all stood silent for a moment as Byron's hate and hopelessness washed over us.

"Who are you really pissed off at?"

Byron scowled at Rick. "What do you mean?"

"Who is ultimately responsible for putting a young boy into that dysfunctional family?"

Byron stood silent for a moment, then glared at Rick. "Damn you to hell!" He spat out, "I hate God! I blame him for my life. I haven't felt him in any way! Fuck God!"

Rick asked Byron to pick a man to play the vengeful part of God who would put a small, defenseless boy into that environment.

Byron gazed around the group and settled on one of the inmates, Robb.

Rick then asked him to pick another man to play a loving God, One who cared for, supported, and loved Byron.

He had a difficult time thinking there might be such a God. Eventually, he chose Sal, one of the staff.

Robb, the vengeful God, was instructed to stand in front of Byron while Sal, the loving God, stood behind him.

"What do you want to say to this vengeful part of God, Byron?"

He folded his arms and scowled at Robb. Then he took a menacing step forward and blurted out, "Fuck you, God! Fuck you for putting me in this family. Fuck you for giving me these useless and abusive parents. Fuck you for leading me to prison! Fuck you! Get out of my life!"

Strangely, the more he raged at this vengeful God, the lighter he became. Finally, after about ten minutes of raging, Byron stopped, exhausted.

"Is all that hate and blame out of your system?" Rick asked.

"Yeah! That was fucking hard. But I feel better now."

Rick told Robb, playing the vengeful God, to walk away. He then said, "Byron, turn around and face Sal. What do you need from this loving God?"

The tall man closed his eyes, then opened them. He stepped forward. "I can't go on like this. I need you in my life."

Sal raised his arms as if to hug Byron. Byron hesitated, then cautiously stepped into Sal's arms. He placed his head on Sal's shoulders and sobbed.

"I love you," said Sal as the loving God. "I always loved you. I'm sorry about what happened to you. You deserved a better childhood."

Byron's sobs intensified. The circle of men watched him transform from a raging maniac into a sweet, loving, spiritual man.

With tears dripping from his face, Byron straightened his back and faced the group. "I feel closer to God than I ever felt in my life. I now feel love in my heart." He appeared shocked himself. "Maybe I can have a spiritual life, 'cause I just felt a miracle."

To those present, that moment did, indeed, feel like a miracle.

Like Byron, some of us have been wounded by religion or have negative associations about spirituality. Some veer toward the secular or profane and profess that spirituality is for wimps, that New Age crap makes men spineless, and that women prefer manly, not saintly, men. Others veer toward the sacred and holy and become involved in religion. What's clear is that a wide range of emotions erupts when people talk about God and spirituality.

We see spirituality as an integral force in men. Ernest Holmes, Founder of Science of Mind, wrote, "There is a living Spirit at the center of your being. The original Author of all life is in and around you." While we echo the belief that we are spiritual beings on a human excursion, we want to clarify our position.

Spirituality has nothing to do with sacred texts, priests, ministers, gurus, churches, commandments, ceremonies, or any of the other trappings to which we so often cling. All these trappings come from man's inherent desire to become more spiritual and to connect to a Higher Power. And these things, which are the mainstays of religion, have often become separated from spiritual practice.

A famous cartoon by Sydney Harris shows two doors. The first one is marked "Heaven," and the second door has the sign "Lecture

About Heaven." The joke follows that the line in front of the second door has a long queue while no one stands before the door to experience heaven directly. Perhaps the people standing in line for the lecture are whom Martin Luther King, Jr. calls "misguided men." He says, "Our scientific power has outrun our spiritual power. We have guided missiles and misguided men."

SPIRITUALITY AND RELIGION

We differentiate religion from spirituality simply: Religion attempts to codify and organize our connection with Spirit, while Spirituality is the direct experience of Spirit we feel in our hearts, soul, and bodies, even our balls. To be clear, we are not denigrating religion. Religion offers connection, community, and devotees whose guidance demonstrates and interprets Spirit's call. Religion often promotes a dualistic approach about body and soul, heaven and earth. This concept separates the physical from the spiritual and creates the appearance that only in death can souls be liberated and experience heaven.

🔘 LEONARD

When I was in eighth grade, I attended a Catholic grammar school and pictured God the father as an elderly man with a white beard, looking down from the sky, who entrusted the Pope and his advisors with the wisdom to hand down rules to keep his flock from sinning. One of the rules I learned was that eating meat on Fridays was forbidden. I never understood the reasoning other than Jesus was crucified on a Friday. What that had to do with fasting from meat always puzzled me. However, I religiously followed that edict to avoid committing a mortal sin, which meant going to hell. Fear motivated me to follow God's command. However, during Vatican II they changed the rule and decreed that Catholics could eat meat on Fridays. That event liberated me. I realized that if I had eaten a hot dog on Friday the previous week, I would have committed a mortal sin and would be absolved only by a priest who listened to my confession. However, after they changed the decree, I could eat hot dogs and burgers on Friday without any pain of sin. From that time forward, I decided that the Pope and his bishops did not have control over my relationship with God.

Many of us yearn for a more direct experience of what we may call Spirit, God, Creative Intelligence, All That Is, Allah, Buddha, Higher Power, Universal Love, or whatever name we choose to call that which is greater than ourselves. As Swami Vivekananda states, "None can make you spiritual. There is no other teacher but your own soul."

Thomas Aquinas described the soul as the ultimate intrinsic source of vital living activity. The word *intrinsic* suggests that it is basic, inherent, and essential. James Thornton, in *A Field Guide to the Soul*, described the soul as "Already fully awakened, perfect, always sustained, unborn, and undying. It knows the sacred in everything."

To be intrinsically connected with the divine is to be Spirit-driven in our interactions and interconnections in the community and with the environment. Our spiritual nature pulsates through us continually and extends outward to others.

Eckhart Tolle, who wrote *A New Earth: Awakening to Your Life's Purpose*, tells us, "That is the real spiritual awakening, when something emerges from within you that is deeper than you thought you were. So, the person is still there, but one could almost say that something more powerful shines through the person."

The benefits of connecting with our spiritual natures are immense. When at home with our spiritual center, we feel loved, cared for, peaceful, and calm. We also enter a state of flow where inner guidance and synchronicity miraculously appear. From that place, our most sacred, radiant parts are revealed, and we become a beacon of light to others. We become the ones we've been waiting for!

We are all called to wake up our spiritual side. Some calls occur after we have crashed and burned and sought inner guidance. Others are less traumatic but powerful, nonetheless.

LEONARD

When I lived in Sydney back in the 80s, I attended a series of meditation classes. After a Sunday intensive with blissful meditation, I returned to my car at 9:30 at night, ready for the thirty-minute drive home. I was in an extremely relaxed state with an open mind. As soon as I started the engine, I received an inner voice instructing me to take a specific route. My judgmental mind hadn't yet kicked into its habitual chattering, so I complied with the request. As I drove, I received further guidance. Actually, a series of instructions periodically altered my course with occasional right and left turns. After twenty minutes, I became impatient and wondered how long the journey would continue. The internal voice, which was calm and loving, immediately replied, "You're almost there." When I approached a two-story red brick house, I was told to slow down and park near the building. Though I was still in a relaxed zone, I became nervous when, after I parked across the street, the internal voice instructed me, "Talk to the people in the house." My judgmental mind immediately responded, "No way!"

As soon as those words entered my mind, however, a young couple stepped out the front door and walked to their car parked near the building.

The voice calmly said, "They are the ones. Talk to them."

I argued back, "What the hell am I supposed to say? That a strange voice asked me to come and speak with you?"

At the time, I worked at a child and adolescent psychiatry department. I knew how I would respond if a patient told me he was hearing internal voices to talk with strangers. My clinical mind took control. I folded my arms around my chest in an act of resistance and refused to budge. I would not talk with them. However, my curiosity had me remain in my car to watch what happened.

The couple had a long discussion by their car and kept looking around as if they were waiting for someone to appear. I kept receiving internal nudges to speak with them, but I resisted. The couple eventually entered their car and drove away. I exhaled a sigh of relief. Then I realized that fear had prevented some holy encounter. Though I had experienced an awakening during the meditation, I had become paralyzed by fear and had fallen back asleep.

During the following week, I pondered that incident. I was upset with myself for not having the courage to follow my internal guidance. Fortunately, lessons repeat themselves. Several weeks later I took a train to work. When a well-dressed man in a gray suit sat next to me, I received another intuitive message, "Speak to him." I initially resisted but, remembering the previous lost opportunity, I said silently, "Give me some help."

No sooner did I hold that thought when the man asked me if there was any good news in the Sydney Morning Herald that I held on my lap. That provided an opening, and before long, our conversation moved to meditation. As it turned out, the man was adept at a particular method of stilling the mind. After sharing his meditation technique, he confided that he was instructed to talk with me. I realized then that all of us receive some form of guidance. Yet we often don't act on it because of fear. When we got off at our stop, we both had twinkles in our eyes as we offered each other a quick handshake.

My encounters in Sydney taught me that we all have an internal GPS. I call my inner GPS, the Guiding Power of Spirit. Whenever, I'm connected with my GPS, I feel inner direction that is calm, peaceful, and loving. My GPS helps me meet the right people at the right time for meaningful exchanges. But I have to stay awake to the ever-present guidance.

When we look divinity straight in the eye and own it, we must courageously face the lies about ourselves contained in any story that we or our families or church have told us that separates us from the truth. As Wayne Dyer states, "We are magnificent, sacred beings." Dr. Dyer didn't mean that we are perfect. Rather, he meant that our essence is divine. Fighting with the darker stories (shadows) we carry only separates us further. So, what is our spiritual work? As spirit-driven men, we can employ power tools to become Spirit-driven. Let's explore them one at a time:

1. UNCOVER THE MESSAGES OR BELIEFS THAT DENY OUR SACREDNESS.

One of the difficult tasks is to uncover the beliefs that tell us we are not spiritual. An American Franciscan friar, Richard Rohr, author of *From Wild Man to Wise Man: Reflections on Male Spirituality*, states, "It is the struggle with darkness and grief that educates the male soul." Our work is to identify and root out messages, stories, or wounds we hold that say we are unloved or unworthy of Divine love. Anything that blocks our grief, anger, or self-love stands in the way of our capacity to connect spiritually with ourselves and others. As we weed out those messages, we recognize our True Selves as spiritual beings on a human excursion.

2. RECOGNIZE THAT WE ARE ON A SACRED HERO'S JOURNEY TO RETURN HOME TO OUR TRUE SELF.

Since all living beings evolve, it stands to reason that spiritual development operates under similar principles. Unless we die prematurely, we transition through birth, childhood, adolescence, adulthood, old age, and death. Each stage follows a blueprint and is necessary for the succeeding phases. We may be at different phases of spiritual development, each following a unique path with individualized lessons, but we are all, nonetheless, climbing that mountain toward Home where we are connected to All That Is.

The following diagram of a flower with six petals highlights the stages of spiritual development: Adaptation, Becoming an Orphan, Wake-up Calls and Signposts, Staying Awake, Healing Wounds and Breaking Free, and Heartbeat of Connection. They lead us Home to the center of the flower which represents the very core of our being, our True Self.

Adaptation marks the stage of being born into a material world and downloading files and programs from our parents, our culture, and society. We construct an identity comprised of these beliefs and adopt roles and behavioral patterns. Over time, we adopt a "false self" separated from our spiritual Home, thereby creating insecurity, anxiety, and fear.

Becoming an Orphan is the next phase of development where we move farthest away from Home, sleepwalking through life, unconscious about our behavioral patterns and the interconnection of life. Orphans wander aimlessly and perceive life from the vantage point of a victim, resigned to an unhappy and often dramatic life of desperation. Homelessness, however, creates a longing to return Home.

Wake-up Calls and Signposts mark the next phase. Our True Self employs a principle of thermodynamics to crack open our unconscious mind. Intense heat generated by traumas and personal crises produces transformation so our eyes can turn inward toward our True Self. Signposts show up along the way and may serendipitously appear in relationships, words, music, symbols, animals, nature, or dreams.

Staying Awake is the next stage of spiritual development. This is often marked by confusion, terror, and anxiety as we face the fear of losing our identity and cherished beliefs. Since an awakened state heightens awareness, we may feel worse as painful memories, long suppressed, are brought to light. However, once we make the declaration to return Home, there's no turning back as we distinguish between life choices that create discord and those that resonate with our True Self.

Healing wounds and Breaking Free mark the time where we begin to heal wounds that create separation and break free from our "False" self. Healing raises our consciousness on the hero's journey toward spirituality. Acceptance and love provide soothing balm as we break free from destructive thoughts, feelings, and behaviors that prevent us from embracing a Spirit-driven life.

Heartbeat of Connection is the stage where we connect with and care for our soul. We consciously attune our life to the powerful principles of Love, Trust, and Self-Mastery and lead a heartfelt and Spirit-driven life dedicated to fulfilling a higher purpose.

The hero's journey of spirituality is a circular process, meaning that we spiral through the stages repeatedly. Repetition brings familiarity. The terrain becomes more recognizable so we can move through the phases with less judgment and more forgiveness. With increased awareness, we steadily integrate spirituality with our human experience. And that takes us to our next Power Tool.

3. MOVE TOWARD A HEALTHIER, INTEGRATED SPIRITUALITY AS WHOLE (HOLY) MEN.

Since we have the capacity to receive unlimited guidance from the Divine, we can utilize six aspects of our lives: an evolving sensory physical body that interacts with the external world, a range of emotions that provides feedback about our internal world, an inquisitive mind that processes information and directs our attention, an open heart that relates with love and compassion, a voice that expresses our inner truth, and a vision that sees the difference between our false self and our True self.

Using a computer analogy, imagine that our spiritual Home represents a wireless connection between our soul and the Divine. We have the capacity to receive unlimited information. The computer frame and motherboard symbolize the physical body while electricity or power represents emotions. The software programs and files signify the mind, and the online social networks represent the realm of relationships. The speakers and keyboard symbolize expression while the screen becomes the symbol for vision. If we neglect or abuse the hardware, disconnect the power source, download viruses and dysfunctional programs, avoid social networks, turn off the sound, disable the keyboard, and shut off the screen, we could never access the wireless connection. Every aspect of the computer is vital.

In a similar fashion, we need a body, feelings, mind, heart, voice, and vision to receive and follow the direction of our True Self. The ego would have us believe that we are our bodies, feelings, and thoughts when in actuality, they are on loan, ours to use just like the computer with all its components. If any realm is shut down, such as our emotions, we limit the inflow and outflow. We don't want to detach but rather strengthen the connection with each facet of our lives. Doing so increases our receptivity to the Divine. We can then hold that Essence as our guiding star each moment of the day.

4. GROW FROM THE INSIDE OUT
THROUGH A DAILY PRACTICE.

Developing a spiritual practice is the fulcrum for our inner work. Our practice is what grounds us, centers us, and humbles us by reminding us that we are part of something far greater than ourselves. It plugs us into an endless source of wisdom, gratitude, connection, forgiveness, and acceptance. There is nothing soft or New Age about a man's spirituality. It is hard won and emanates from within.

Real spiritual work is not an airy-fairy, pseudo-spiritual process, nor is it for the faint of heart. It takes a lifetime to complete, for it challenges belief systems or doctrines that try to make us unholy, defective sinners.

We do not advocate a particular practice, only one that aligns with who you are. Develop a practice that you can use daily. If you have one that works for you already, great. If not, experiment with some of the methods of spiritual traditions. Meditation and prayer are common in most traditions, and they come in many different flavors. Other practices include journaling, time in nature, transformational trainings, twelve-step work, contemplation, breath work, and a daily ritual of expressing gratitude.

We do not put spiritual practices into some hierarchy. No one practice or technique is greater, more sacred, or higher than another. Each can lead to greater awareness and self-realization if we persevere over time. Hence, once you establish a practice, continue with it for at least three weeks and then evaluate if it fits you. Avoid struggling with spirituality, and if you can, have some fun with it.

RICK

I've been doing my spiritual practice for more than sixty years. Each morning, I do conscious breathing (Rebirthing breaths or Yogic Kriya breaths); then I meditate for twenty to thirty minutes in silence. While meditating, I focus on being grateful for all the good things I have been given. I also send love to my loved ones and dear friends and to my enemies as well! I say my Golden and Dark Shadow Missions to myself every day to remind myself why I am on this planet and set my intentions for the day. (See Chapter Eight on Mission.) Sometimes, I add journaling, reading, visualizations, and quiet time in nature as part of my practice on an as needed basis. Even riding my Harley can be a spiritual experience!

When I do my practice, I start the day feeling grateful, grounded, loving, peaceful, and thankful. All these feelings lead me to a productive, joyful day. These techniques also help me through any challenging events. I can't imagine my day without this practice!

LEONARD

Forty years ago, I attended a meditation course. The instructor told me that if I meditated every day for six months, it would change my life. I was skeptical but gave it a shot. Sure enough, it did change my life, so much so that not meditating when I wake up feels like skipping breakfast. Another practice that fuels my soul is writing. I have banker's boxes filled with journals that include my thoughts, feelings, and dreams. When I feel connected with Spirit, my most creative writing occurs as I tune into creativity and a Higher Consciousness.

While both of those practices are solitary, I try and look for spiritual connections with others. Doing this brings me tremendous spiritual rewards.

Ten years ago, I visited my 96-year-old mother on Mother's Day. At the time, she resided in a nursing home in Ohio near my sister and brother-in-law. Though she had dementia, my mother appeared to watch the world through the sparking eyes of an innocent child.

During my visit, I wondered if she recognized me, so I asked her if I was her brother, her son, or her father. She thought a moment, then responded with utmost confidence, "You are all of them." She obviously knew about Oneness of Spirit.

I asked her if she knew my name. She paused again and then answered, "Acceptance."

Dementia may have caused my mother to lose her rational faculties, but she had not lost contact with Spirit. Her spirit-driven message to me was clear. Practice Acceptance.

AN ATTITUDE OF GRATITUDE AS A SPIRITUAL PRACTICE

"It is through gratitude for the present moment that the spiritual dimension of life opens up."

— *Eckhart Tolle*

Throughout time, spiritual teachers and texts have reminded us of the value of living in gratitude. We echo that call and invite men to embrace gratitude. Here is a simple practice:

- Notice where you are blessed and the gifts that have been bestowed on you for no other reason than you exist.

- Notice how you are supported in mysterious ways.

- Notice where you have abundance.

- Notice the sacred and beautiful relations with family, friends, coworkers, and even strangers.

If you can do this, you will find happiness and spiritual peace. You will find grace in everything you do, even when the task is unpleasant or difficult. As the motivational speaker Denis Waitley says, "Happiness cannot be traveled to, owned, earned, worn, or consumed. Happiness is the spiritual experience of living every minute with love, grace, and gratitude."

5. CONNECT WITH ELDERS IN A SPIRITUAL COMMUNITY.

While discussing Spirituality, which is often a personal experience, we want to stress the important Power Tool of sharing spirituality in community. Buddhists use the word *sangha* to describe a community of fellow practitioners. Spiritual practice can be more easily done when elders play a role in the spiritual development of younger men. The Franciscan Richard Rohr writes, "No civilization has ever survived unless the elders saw it as their duty to pass on gifts of Spirit to the young ones."

A man's spiritual journey involves the transmittance of wisdom and experience from older to younger men. At one time, the elders in the tribe were revered for their knowledge. The younger men were hungry to hear their stories and feed their souls. Sharing the sacred stories was about passing down soulful tradition and helping the tribe survive.

Awakened men become the elders in the community. We have a responsibility to tell our stories, even our messiness, as we share our spiritual lessons gleaned from our journey to answer calls, climb

111

mountains, overcome crashes, and reach crests. Stories of our triumphs and disasters, insights and ignorance, and dark shadows and gold can inspire and motivate other men to become spirit-driven.

We, Rick and Leonard, have heard countless stories of men who never received sustaining fathering or mentoring. The "father wound" of these men made spiritual mentoring especially crucial for advancing into healthy manhood. We continually receive feedback about how honestly sharing our stories from a vulnerable place inspires other men to open up and face their challenges, mistakes, and setbacks.

Diving into our spiritual journeys, we can find the joy, gratitude, and gravitas that help us become the potent and sacred elders. From that place, we will feel deep in our bones that we are spiritual beings and can let our light radiate freely with open hearts and souls in the pursuit of *whole-iness*.

Having covered Connection, Love, Authenticity, and Spirituality in the CLASSICS Model, we are ready to embrace our **Sexuality**.

STRETCH YOURSELF SPIRITUALLY

1. Think of a time when you were angry with God. What were the circumstances? How did you resolve your feelings?

2. Experiment with a new spiritual practice for three weeks. Notice how you feel while practicing. Notice what messages come up regarding your sacredness or holiness.

3. Journal for several days about self-love. Pay attention to any messages that seem to refute your essential goodness. Notice where these messages originally came from.

4. Attend a transformational workshop that stretches you and your beliefs about yourself. Surrender to the experience. Notice any transformation that occurs during the process.

5. Keep a Gratitude Journal. Write each day what you're thankful for, whether those items or incidents be big or small. Spend a few minutes writing about how existence supports you during the day.

6. Find an elder or a community with whom you could share stories or experiences about your spiritual journey. Share the darkness and the light of your journey.

7. Find a younger man to whom you could offer eldering.

Chapter Seven

Build a Healthy Sexual Life

Sexuality is one of the ways we become enlightened, actually, because it leads to self-knowledge.

— Alice Walker

O ur penises are so damned mysterious, aren't they? How our genitals work—or don't work—fascinates, scares, and confuses us. We are terrified that we are not masculine enough, hard enough, big enough, last long enough, or "hetero" enough. We take substances to get or maintain a hard-on. We rely on other substances to put us in the mood or calm us down. We masturbate addictively or don't masturbate at all, due to the many messages we received as children. We have affairs with men and women, watch porn secretly, brag to other men about our supposed sexual conquests, perhaps become asexual completely, and never, ever, speak authentically about our sexual selves. Why?

Very few of us have had the benefit of being raised with a healthy attitude toward sex. We often put our base instincts into shadow. However, when we do that, we can act out in destructive, hurtful ways such as sexual abuse of children, overuse of porn, self-abuse, and prostitution.

Our goal is to open up a conversation with men about our sexuality that is sacred, honest, loving, and authentic. We want to learn how to build authentic and healthy sexuality, yet there isn't a subject more fraught with difficulty, pitfalls, and shame for us men than sexuality. We posture, lie about our sexual conquests, and magnify our sexual power and potency even as we are completely mystified, terrified, and ignorant of our own sexual natures. And then we can berate another man by using sexual terms like *prick*, *cocksucker*, or *dickhead*.

While we receive our beliefs about sexuality from our family and culture, considerable shaming and trauma often come from our religious upbringing. Yet, how can we believe that our bodies, especially our penises, are ugly or harmful when we were created in His image, according to the Bible and other sacred texts?

🜂 RICK

I sat in the circle of twenty-five naked men on a weekend in 1990 as we shared our stories of sexual wounding. We had been invited to voluntarily take off our clothes on the third day of this weekend experience as a way to build intimacy and safety about this topic. When it was my turn to share, my stomach did back flips. I had never told my story before, so I was ashamed and scared—no, terrified—to talk about my body. As the last male in my high school to grow hair on my balls, I was teased, shamed, and bullied. Compounding the problem, my penis was on the smaller side, and my mother, a rape survivor, laid a strong religious trip on me and my sibs about the dangerousness and sinfulness of our sexuality.

I shared this with the men in my circle, surprised at how compassionately they listened. My shame had debilitated me so much that it had become almost impossible for me to piss in public. I was terrified that another man would look over the urinal and judge me less than a man.

I looked around the circle of men and saw heads nod in understanding. After everyone had shared their sexual wounds, pain, and confusion, the facilitator of the group asked us to stand up.

"Take a good look around, men," he said. "I know you want to!"

Many laughed. I complied and noticed a variety of penises, some larger, a few smaller, some darker in color, others lighter, some circumcised, others not. Yet, all were beautiful in their own way. I felt incredibly liberated! Since that day, I have not had an issue peeing in public.

We deserve to love our bodies, access pleasure, and sexually express ourselves responsibly. Our partners deserve our respect and appreciation for their bodies. Yet, we often disconnect bodies and souls from sexual expression, thereby focusing only on orgasmic release. This has a tremendous cost for us and our lovers.

THE SPLIT BETWEEN SEXUALITY AND SPIRITUALITY

Most of us instinctively feel a deep divide between our sexuality and our spirituality. They seem to be mutually exclusive, even antagonistic. This divide causes us to hide, repress, and deny our sexuality, especially if our urges are different from the monogamous, heterosexual, marriage-oriented norms. We stuff our sexual urges into shadow (as described in Chapter Five) because we were taught early on that they were somehow bad, abusive, or evil. These beliefs are still taught routinely by many of our churches and other groups. Religious prohibitions establish many of our societal/cultural sexual mores, resulting in being told what *not* to do with our sexuality. Rarely are we taught that sexual expression can be creative, expressive, joyful, and soulful.

 LEONARD

I spent eight years in the Catholic seminary—four years in high school and four years in college. During that time, I heard only one lecture about sexuality, and that came from a priest who was so nervous he had to frequently stop and use a handkerchief to wipe the sweat pouring down his face. Therefore, my limited knowledge of sex came from the streets of Chicago where I learned the "dirty" secrets from my friends who were just as ignorant as I was.

When I eventually left the seminary, I became involved with my future wife, Marylou, a good Catholic woman. Still a virgin at twenty-one, I was totally unprepared for sex. My first experience having intercourse did not produce fireworks. Rather, it fizzled into a humiliating act of incompetence. Initially, I was so nervous, I couldn't get an erection. Marylou didn't have much sexual experience herself and asked what was wrong. Fortunately, she understood my anxiety because after I achieved an erection, she became nervous herself and wasn't sufficiently lubricated for me to penetrate. We took the time to talk about our sexual lives, or lack thereof, and laugh at our inexperience. As we both relaxed, we became more sexual. I became erect, she lubricated, and I penetrated. Hooray, or so I thought. But nothing happened. It wasn't until the next day that I realized I needed to thrust in and out. (God, was I naïve!) After more discussions and experimentations, we finally experienced fireworks!

Though my first experience with sex didn't create a hallelujah, it did create a genuine moment of intimacy where Marylou and I not only became vulnerable but didn't shame each other. That opened the door for deeper conversations and shared sexual intimacy. Amazing grace!

GENDER IDENTITY

Back in the fifties when Alfred Kinsey published his seminal work on human sexuality, our culture became aware of the hurtful confines that our binary thinking about gender creates. No longer are we limited to just male-female or straight-gay dichotomies. Today, a vast range of gender and sexual expression is being recognized and slowly accepted, especially with millennials. The former constraining gender box is now expanded into a panoply of terms and expressions that attempt to qualify, if not quantify, that range of gender and sexual expression. Sexual orientation is whom I go to bed with; Gender identity is who I go to bed as. They are not the same but need to be better understood.

Straight, gay, lesbian, queer, questioning, gender fluid, asexual, gender neutral, and transgender are a few of the many designations researchers and experts employ to understand gender and sexuality. Gone are the simple days of just male and female, and just straight and gay as categories. Thank goodness. Awakened men have the opportunity and tools to explore their sexuality and identity in ways that were unthinkable to our fathers.

As cisgendered (term given those of us whose gender identity matches our sex assigned at birth), hetero men, we authors do not claim to be experts on issues of orientation or gender identity. However, we have worked with many men and women who claim many of the categories outlined above. We also recognize the incredible pain of not fitting into the binary model and the cost, even today, of coming out and publicly owning any non-binary gender identity or any non-hetero orientation or transgendered identity. We have worked with gay men who married women, either as an attempt to prove their masculinity or to fit into a society that denigrates and demonizes homosexuality. This decision resulted in great damage to these men, their children, and their partners. Coming to terms with their oppression, choices, and the impacts they had on their loved ones took some of these men years to face their pain and reclaim their own sexuality. In addition, we have close transgendered friends who have suffered severe abuse and fear for their lives because they choose to live as the gender that matches their inner identity.

We support our brothers who identify as non-heterosexual or non-binary. We support our transgendered brothers (and sisters!) and believe that our CLASSICS Model offers them a path for integration, growth, and evolution. We support everyone coming to terms with both their gender identity and their sexual orientation so we can all build better lives!

In confronting these issues, we recognize the sexual/spiritual split that pervades our culture. Early on, churches purposely worked to legislate sexual behavior. Those attempts became encoded into organized religions as rules, commandments, or strong mores that differentiated the blessed from the sinner. Sex outside of marriage, contraception, divorce, abortion, same-sex love, and other behaviors was forbidden for those who wished to be acceptable in the eyes of God and the church community. These rules resulted in a restricted, vanilla, man-on-top sexuality (it's even called the *missionary* position!). This procreative brand of sexuality severely stunted our growth and exploration and branded many as unacceptable and even evil.

🌀 LEONARD

Many years ago when I lived in Australia, I taught a five-week couple's course for a Catholic counseling organization. One of the topics focused on ways couples could improve their sexual relationship. That included pleasuring techniques that enhanced a couple's lovemaking. The bishop heard about the course and berated the director of the agency who had hired me to run the program. According to the bishop, the focus of sex had to be on procreation. Obviously, the bishop, with his vow of celibacy, wasn't interested in couples' pleasure. When the red-faced director asked me to scrap the section on sexuality, I told her to get someone else to teach the course. If the couples followed the bishop's rules, they would miss out on the sacred act of a soulful sexual communion.

RICK

Recently, my partner, Michele, and I were traveling with a group in another country. Two of the travelers included Gina, a vibrant, attractive twenty-four-year-old woman with Pete, her husband of six years. Gina knew that Michele, who's a certified sex coach, and I coached other couples about sexuality.

While the group waited for a delayed flight, she awkwardly approached me with a question, "What do you do with a man who doesn't satisfy his partner and who won't talk about it? My husband doesn't understand foreplay. He lasts a short time during intercourse. I don't enjoy sex anymore and don't know what to do. Please help!"

When I asked Gina if she talked to her husband about her feelings, she replied, "Yes, but he has no understanding of what to do. He can't even talk about our sex life. If I raise the topic, he shuts down and sulks for days. I avoid talking about it now."

I asked her if her husband ever shared what turned him on or felt good?

She shook her head. "He won't discuss it."

"Do you ever try oral sex or other ways of pleasing each other?"

"No way! We only do it in the missionary position."

I tried another tack, "Does your husband masturbate?"

She looked horrified. "I've never asked, and he wouldn't answer if I did. In fact, I have never seen him masturbate, nor has he seen me." She then pleaded with me, "Could you talk to my husband and share our conversation about sex?"

With this couple, I felt deep sadness that they could not share their sexual feelings, desires, and needs. Obviously, they needed education about healthy sexuality. I suggested marriage counseling, but she said her husband had rejected that idea.

I told Gina, "If I approach Pete without his permission, it will cause more shame and shut him down. Besides, you both need to work on this issue. Talk to my partner about your concerns, woman to woman.

Michele has lots of experience helping women in your situation. And when Pete opens up, he could reach out to me for some ideas."

Gina did speak to Michele, who gave her helpful advice, but, sadly, neither of us heard from Gina or Pete again. I have had conversations like this with men and women of different ages, nationalities, and races, and feel sad and angry when I hear about the damage that some of our religious and cultural teachings have had on our sexuality.

We echo the legendary pop singer Prince when he said, "I've always understood the two to be intertwined: sexuality and spirituality. That never changed." We, therefore, become enlightened when we expand our knowledge of sexuality. David Deida, renowned for his work with men, wrote *Finding God Through Sex: A Spiritual Guide to Ecstatic Loving and Deep Passion for Men and Women.* He says, "You can open to God through sex. By learning to open your heart and body while embracing and trusting all energies, from rough ravishment to sublime gentleness, you can open to be lived by the mystery that lives the entire universe."[31]

When we spontaneously say, "Oh, God," while having an orgasm, we are not just rejoicing because we've come. We are acknowledging something sacred. The French call it the *petit mort*, the small death. Sex opens the door to the physical release of tension as well as an opening to pleasure and connection to self and another in mystical ways. Cynthia Bourgeault in *Love Is Stronger Than Death* writes, "Erotic love is a holy gift of God. And sometimes this love is so intense and powerful, and the sense of union so strong, that it continues right on growing beyond the grave, knitting two souls into the one wholeness they were always intended to become."[32]

---

31   Deida, David, *Finding God Through Sex: A Spiritual Guide to Ecstatic Loving and Deep Passion for Men and Women,* Plexus, 2002, pp. vii.

32   Bourgeault, Cynthia, *Love Is Stronger Than Death,* Praxis Publishing, New York, 2008.

Acknowledging and exploring this holiness is a clear way to build a better, more loving and more pleasurable life.

Patricia Albere elaborated this concept in *Evolutionary Relationships*. She poignantly writes, "When two souls make love from this state of passion, there is an intuitive sense that what flows through you is a sacred energy that somehow benefits much more than just you and your partner."[33]

Clearly, limiting our sexual expression curbs our emotional and spiritual development as men. Before we delve deeper into how an awakened, evolving man finds and reclaims that connection between his authentic, vital sexuality and his spirituality, let's first explore how we got here.

HOW DID WE GET THIS WAY?

Author Steve Bearman, in his article, "Why Are Men So Obsessed with Sex," states, "... from the moment of our birth, if not earlier, we are treated as gendered beings. We are not merely considered to have a gender, we are conditioned to have it. Moment by moment, day by day, and persistently over long stretches of time, the ways boys and girls get treated shape their identities."[34]

Most cultures treat their boys in a way that leads males to cut off from their feelings, their bodies, and their authentic sexuality. As a result, men repress sensuality, deny feelings, and go numb, as a matter of course. These behavioral patterns may have prepared men to battle the elements of the world and even to go to war. Soldiers are prepared to use their bodies and their lives in defense of country, family, and women and children.

Numbing begins shortly after birth with male circumcision. Up until recently, men in the west were routinely circumscribed,

---

33 Albere, Op. Cit., pp. 217.

34 Bearman, Steve, "Why Are Men So Obsessed with Sex," *Elephant Journal*, October 13, 2013.

mostly for religious reason, or because parents believed that a circumcised penis was healthier. This act, done within a few days of birth without any anesthetic while the baby boy is strapped down, spread-eagled on a board, is considered barbaric by many, including our friend and fellow writer, Jed Diamond, who states the following about circumcision in *The Warrior's Journey Home: Healing Men, Healing the Planet:*

- "The traumatic and long-lasting effects of circumcision on the male infant occur before language development. Therefore, it's difficult for men to remember what happened and heal their emotional scars.

- The abusive act of circumcision can contribute to later problems with addiction and violence. Therefore, ending this practice can help ensure that the next generation of boys has a chance to grow up healthy and free."[35]

As Diamond states, whether they know it or not, circumcised men carry the trauma of having a piece of their penis cut off and discarded. Desensitizing the delicate nerves lessens the sensitivity of the penis and adds to our physical numbness, which only deepens our emotional numbness. Unless parents are members of a religion that requires circumcision, we don't advocate it as it disconnects us from our genitals.

Zeke, a twenty-seven-year-old married man, was unequivocal about his feelings about circumcision. His Jewish parents made the difficult decision not to circumcise him, even though many in their culture found this unacceptable. "I'm so glad my parents didn't circumcise me!" said Zeke. "It seems like a barbaric act. I feel like a whole man and am glad of it. I've read that without the protection

---

35 Diamond, Jed, *The Warrior's Journey Home: Healing Men, Healing the Planet,* New Harbinger Publications, Oakland, CA, 1994, pp. 141.

of the foreskin, the head of the penis loses some of its pleasurable sensitivity. I can't say for sure, since I've never experienced what it's like, but I certainly enjoy my sensitivity. My wife does, too!"

Well-known family therapist and author, Terrence Real, in a recent webinar for mental health professionals stated that the way we turn boys into men in our culture is through trauma and disconnection. If he is right, then the quest for men to have meaningful and fulfilling sex lives is through the healing of that trauma and disconnection, which starts literally and sadly at birth.

We have heard countless stories from lonely men who have numbed their bodies and emotions and deadened the feelings of pleasure. This lack of feeling can lead us to devalue our sexual partners, which can result in harassment or sexual abuse at the personal level and sustaining the patriarchy at the cultural level.

THE SETUP FOR COMPULSIVE SEXUAL BEHAVIOR STARTS EARLY

Author Steve Bearman writes, "… boys are encouraged to develop relationships with other boys that are primarily competitive: playing sports, jockeying for higher rank in social hierarchies such as teams, clubs, and later on, gangs and fraternities. These groups often come together to do violence to other groups, either by 'beating' them in competitions or in less symbolic forms of violence."[36]

While growing up as boys, we learned to disconnect from emotions through structured, competitive games that valued accomplishment and achievement. This type of disconnection often gets transferred to the area of sex where performance and ejaculation become the gold standard versus the enjoyment of sensual pleasure. As Judith Jordon, one of the creators of Relational-Cultural Theory, writes, "Women are often attuned to and want sensitivity to feeling, while men tend to focus more on action.… When

---

36 Bearman, Op. Cit.

sexuality becomes mechanical meeting directed toward orgasmic discharge only, a performance of the ego or narcissistic exercise of the self, a conquest of one by another, it becomes one of the most profoundly lonely and limiting experiences."[37]

Bearman also posits that this conditioning leaves us prone to sexual obsession because during sex, men are (at last!) allowed to feel. We yearn to feel, so we seek out the only societally acceptable way for us to safely feel—through sex. As Steve Bearman and others have pointed out, men in particular are set up for compulsive sexual behavior or unhealthy sexual behavior.

Adolescent boys are bombarded by sexual images through TV, advertising, websites, and magazines. All this while their bodies are fueled by an increase of testosterone. Many of these images convey that life is not complete or enjoyable unless one is having sex. Add in the message that we must *get laid* to prove our masculinity— long before we even know what *getting laid* even means—we may feel the pressure to become sexual way before we're emotionally ready. Then we have to battle crazy, mixed messages, one from church and society that states that sex should be saved for true love and marriage, and another from Hollywood that macho men get their women.

Here's the catch, again according to Bearman, "… sexuality genuinely can be a potent source of love and pleasure, intimacy, sensuality, and beauty. But in no way, can sex completely fulfill these needs. Such needs can only be fulfilled by healing from the effects of male conditioning and suffusing every area of our lives with relatedness and aliveness."[38]

Most of us first learned about sex by masturbating as teenagers (unless you attended a seminary)! Jerking off was purely physical with ejaculation as the primary goal. David Deida tells us in

---

37 Jordan, Judith, et. al., *Women's Growth in Connection: Writings from the Stone Center*, Guilford Press, New York, 1991, pp. 89-90.

38 Bearman, Op. Cit.

Finding God Through Sex that for a man, "Love is something that happens in his heart. Sex is something that happens with his genitals. Most men find it easy to enjoy one without the other, which is reflected in the popularity of girlie magazines and prostitution."[39] This phenomenon can lead to misogyny and support patriarchy.

CREATION OF PATRIARCHY AND MISOGYNY

The patriarchy that seems to run invisibly (at least for many of us men) was created for a reason, we believe! It was designed to desensitize men, so our bodies and souls became numb. We become better soldiers when this occurs. We were also conditioned to be dominant over other men, women, children, and the planet. We were taught to value winning over cooperation and to never admit our weaknesses or insecurities. We perpetuate that patriarchal thinking and system when we do not question it.

How did this system start? Feminist writer, bell hooks, shares these powerful words: "The first act of violence that patriarchy demands of males is not violence toward women. Instead patriarchy demands of all males that they engage in acts of psychic self-mutilation, that they kill off the emotional parts of themselves. If an individual is not successful in emotionally crippling himself, he can count on patriarchal men to enact rituals of power that will assault his self-esteem."

Just take a moment and really read and absorb hooks' words. They bring tears of recognition of the pain that this system of male dominance foists on us men and then tears at how we pass that pain onto others—especially women. We want to be clear that we are not blaming men for this system. That very psychic self-mutilation that hooks speaks of cuts us off from much that makes us men human. This system predated our existence on the planet, yet we continue to benefit from and perpetuate it and be harmed by

---

39   Deida, Op. Cit., p. 9.

it—all at the same time. We believe this system also creates the environment for sexual harassment and sows the seeds for the behaviors that led to the #MeToo movement. It is this system that must be challenged.

SEXUAL HARASSMENT AND THE #METOO MOVEMENT

The recent societal upheaval occurring around revelations of male sexual harassment in the film industry, government, and the corporate world highlights men's responsibility to be clear about sexual intentions and to listen carefully to a partner's wants and needs.

Rick is a member of Sex Positive San Diego (with chapters around the US) that teaches clear and simple rules to gain authentic consent from a potential sex partner. His trainer and friend, Dr. Jen Gunsaullus, clearly states the issue of consent: "If you don't get to a *Hell Yes*, then the answer is a *NO!*" The Power Tool of getting to a "Hell Yes!" is so valuable.

When our sexuality operates from shadow, we act out on women (or other men) by ignoring the words or signs of a *NO!* Not getting a *Hell Yes* causes incalculable pain, disconnection, and mistrust. CLASSICS Men recognize the responsibility to achieve clarity, gain clear consent from a partner, establish boundaries, and prevent abuse. Personal boundaries involve an awareness of what is acceptable and unacceptable as well as an obligation to make healthy choices.

We believe it is critical to learn to stop bullying partners, objectifying them, and taking advantage of power differentials for our own gratification at the expense of others. We also urge other men to do the same and to become allies to women and LGBTQ+ folks. We can and should work tirelessly to address harassment and sexual abuse in the world. We can do this by taking the following steps to prevent the sexual harassment, rape, and mistreatment of women:

1. We own our sexism/misogyny with other men.

2. We catalog the damage and pain that this system has foisted on us as men.

3. We go inward and rescript the messages we were given that women are "less than" men.

4. We practice loving and accepting the feminine parts of ourselves.

5. We actively interrupt other men when they put down women or act out on them.

Both of us practice these steps regularly with ourselves and the men with whom we work. An ongoing commitment and practice produce transformation that expands our sexual expression to be a joyful and sacred experience for all.

THE DECLARATION OF MALE SEXUAL RIGHTS POWER TOOL

Many men have been taught that they do not have the right to enjoy their sexuality freely. This has caused us to create an important Power Tool we call the "Declaration of Male Sexual Rights."

Men have these rights:

1. Be inherently sexual, erotic beings who embrace our healthy sexuality, no matter our age or orientation.

2. Feel safe in sexual relationships.

3. Connect our sexuality with our hearts and souls.

4. Receive joy, aliveness, and connection from authentic sexual expression.

5. Freely explore our own truths about our sexual expression, what turns us on and what is playful, fun, and erotic between consenting adults.

6. Need other men with whom we can openly share our thoughts and feelings about sexual problems, pain, issues, joys, or passions.

7. Create a strong, heartfelt sexual connection with ourselves which makes our connection with our partners more fulfilling and resilient.

8. Be celibate or asexual without shame.

We urge all men to fully embrace our sexual rights. As mentioned earlier, we awaken our masculine sexual selves by expanding our senses, opening our hearts, and embracing our feelings. These often involve *surrendering*, not a popular word with men. Surrendering in sexuality means letting go of our need to perform and reach the finish line of ejaculation. Surrendering asks us to relax into the moment and allow sensations, movement, and sounds to emerge without judgment.

We may notice how sensitive our nipples or lips can be. We may want to emit a guttural sound or dance in ecstasy while making love. We may tune into our partner's pleasure in new and unexpected ways. We may discover delicious feelings that have otherwise gone unnoticed. Senses even change while making love. We may taste and smell and hear differently. As we remain open and mindful of the freshness of each moment, we fill our cup with the sweet nectar of sacred, sensuous love. This is Godly, kingly in our judgment!

SELF-PLEASURING POWER TOOL

One way for men to practice becoming more proficient and open lovers is to embrace the Power Tool of self-pleasure. Most males masturbate at some point in their lives. Young boys may play with their genitals to the point of arousal. Parents often become uncomfortable with their children's natural sexual curiosity and promote guilt and shame. If we were suppressed as children, we probably will hold a residue of shame when we pleasure ourselves. Strangely, men often aren't very good at self-pleasure. We may use erotic pictures or pornography for stimulation; however, that path may turn others into objects to satisfy our own pleasure.

The derogatory connotation ascribed to words like *dick*, *cock*, *pussy*, and *cunt* take away from the beautiful gift of experiencing that parts of our bodies provide us with immense pleasure that can be shared. If we want to be good lovers, we have to learn how to love ourselves. That includes loving our genitals.

Margo Anand, author of *The Art of Sexual Ecstasy*, writes, "... the negative ideas associated with masturbation need to be healed. That is why I have replaced *masturbation* with the term *self-pleasuring*. Masturbation has something cold and clinical about it, something furtive and shameful that separates people from their hearts and prevents self-acceptance. Self-pleasuring, on the other hand, implies that it is good and healthy for the self to be pleasured, celebrated, and enjoyed. It also suggests that the whole body is involved, not just one part of it."[40]

Anand recommends that we consciously learn how to pleasure ourselves by learning about the different kinds of touches, positions, breathing, fantasies, and music that can intensify our pleasure which we can then contain and feel more deeply. Self-pleasuring becomes a practice of increasing arousal, delaying release by stopping before ejaculation, then building up the arousal again. The goal isn't necessarily ejaculation, though that may happen, but to ride the waves of pleasure to increase staying power. When we do let go, the ejaculation becomes more intense and pleasurable.

---

40 Anand, Margo, *The Art of Sexual Ecstasy: The Path of Sacred Sexuality for Western Lovers*, Jeremy Tarcher, Los Angeles, 1989, p. 196.

🌑 LEONARD

Many years ago, Margo Anand's books introduced me to self-pleasuring. Like most men, I had been embarrassed about talking to anyone about masturbating except in a humorous way. Even as I write this, I feel some embarrassment about what you, the reader, might think. So, let's get this out of the way. I enjoy self-pleasure! Since I'm not currently in a relationship, I'm grateful to have the ability to experience sexual pleasure. My journey has been hard fought ever since I left the seminary (or sexual cemetery).

So what did I do? I followed the Self-Pleasuring Rituals in Anand's book. I established a sacred space and time where I would not be interrupted. During my one-hour "practice period," I would expand my sense of touch and discover my body. My goal wasn't to ejaculate but to learn how to create waves of pleasure by exploring, arousing areas of my body, stopping, then arousing other responsive parts. I discovered sensitive nipples, something many men wouldn't even consider. I also learned how to ride the waves of pleasure so they could be sustained over longer periods of time. And when I became involved with a lover, I brought my skills to the relationship. I've come a long way from being an asexual seminarian, and, thank God, I still have heaps to learn!

Consider developing your own practice of self-pleasuring. Notice what areas of your body feel good and any emotions that come up. Find a safe circle of friends or other men with whom you could share your revelations. You'll be amazed at what you'll discover. Once the doors are open to talk about sex, you will hear both sad and humorous stories. Some may talk about the pain of living in a sexless marriage or about erectile dysfunction. Others will laugh at the bullshit they were taught when in grammar school, such as masturbation and wet dreams would send them to hell. Feeling comfortable talking about our sex begins with sharing our own stories.

Fortunately, expanding our sexuality never has to stop. In fact, we can become better lovers of ourselves and our partner, even as we age. Psychologist Dr. David Schnarch states in *Passionate Marriage*, "... feelings and thoughts must replace biological drives and sensory awareness as the major determinants of your sexuality. Exploring your sexual potential isn't just easier to do; it's a necessity if you want to keep sex a vital part of your life as you get older."[41] Schnarch goes on to affirm that if we are dependent on our sex drives alone to get us started, sex will inevitably drop off as we age. Why? Our horniness hormones diminish as we get older.

Does that mean that sexual connection must also diminish? Of course not! There obviously are differences in our sexuality as we age. However, there are advantages to aging that make good sex even more accessible. With age we require more stimulation to reach orgasm. Therefore, we can last longer and give and receive more pleasure. We can choose to keep the sexual fires lit and add fun to our sensual exploration by adding erotic exploration and expression to our sexuality. This is a Power Tool that keeps on giving!

Schnarch, Esther Perel, and other writers in the sexuality field advocate erotic connections that bring juice and aliveness to our partnerships. Schnarch states, "Eroticism is what turns you on. It makes sex personal, electric, and—well, *sexy*. Eroticism lives in the tone and nuance of sex, the way you engage your partner. It's about where your head's at more than what your genitals do."[42]

The most important sex organ is our brain. As Esther Perel, an international advisor on sex and relationships, writes, "The central agent of eroticism is the human imagination."[43] We invite you to

41 Schnarch, Dr. David, *Passionate Marriage: Love, Sex and Intimacy in Emotionally Committed Relationships*, W.W. Norton and Co., New York, 1997, p. 89.

42 Schnarch, Op. Cit., p. 90.

43 Perel, Esther, *Mating in Captivity: Unlocking Erotic Intelligence*, Harper, New York, 2007, p. 109.

consider these questions from your head, rather than from your genitals:

- What parts of your sexuality have you buried, judged, or ignored? At what cost?

- When you have sex, what does your heart want?

- How can you bring love and fun into your bedroom?

- How can you and your partner reconnect your sacred selves with your sexual selves?

- What secret desires do you harbor that you want to explore?

- What erotic stories turn you and your partner on?

- How can you both play with your erotic selves in a way that spices up your connection?

An array of literature, toys, tools, and DVDs exist to explore your erotic selves so you can reignite your and your partner's sexual flames. Erotic exploration together deepens and strengthens bonds. Sounds like fun, doesn't it?

We're aware that we would need a book of its own to even begin to fully cover masculine sexuality. As we stated at the beginning of this chapter, our goal was to start a conversation and hope that you will continue it with others. Our sacred and powerful masculine sexuality can serve us and our partners as we strive to keep love, sexuality, spiritual connection, and playfulness paramount in our relationships. We invite all men to embrace their Male Sexual Rights. Through those clear statements and greater awareness, we encourage a shameless pathway that fosters an evolved, juicier, and healthier expression of our sensual, sexual selves.

Now that we've covered five dimensions of the CLASSICS Model—connection, love, authenticity, spirituality, and sexuality—we are ready to embody the sixth dimension of **Intention**.

THE SEXUAL STRETCH

We've included a longer list of questions that cover an array of sexual issues. You can journal the answers or discuss them with a partner, close friend, men's group, or therapist.

1. Describe your first sexual experience. How old were you?

2. How many sex partners have you had? Male? Female?

3. Do love and sex need to go together? Explain.

4. What did you always want to know about sex but were afraid to ask?

5. Name the erotic areas of your body.

6. Do you think your penis is small, medium, large, or extra-large? How do you feel about it?

7. What do you think and feel about your partner's genitals?

8. What is your biggest fear about sex?

9. What do you feel ashamed about with sex?

10. Describe how you make love. What's your favorite part?

11. What gives you the most sexual pleasure?

12. How do you feel about oral, vaginal, and/or anal sex? Giving? Receiving?

13. What does a partner do that really turns you on?

14. What haven't you tried in sex that you would like to?

15. Describe one of your favorite sexual fantasies?

16. What have you never told anyone about sex?

17. What have you always wanted to ask a partner to do in sex but never asked?

18. Name a sexual secret.

Chapter Eight

Build a Life of Intention with a Mission

The way you get meaning in your life is to devote yourselves to loving others, devote yourself to your community around you, and devote yourself to something that gives you purpose and meaning.

— Mitch Albom

When he was a sophomore in high school, Nicholas, one of Rick's former students, contracted leukemia. He faced near death and was miraculously saved by a bone marrow transplant. After spending a painful junior year healing, Nicholas became healthy enough to complete school. Near the end of his senior year, he joined Rick's ten-day backpacking science trip that took place every summer. It incorporated mission work along with science activities in beautiful Kettle Moraine State Park in central Wisconsin.

At the end of a long day of hiking, the students, who were fifteen to eighteen years old, sat around the campfire to create Missions of Service. The process had them identify their vision and then clarify their action. In other words, they were asked to recognize and answer the call to climb their mountain.

During the process, Nicholas burst into tears. He leaned on the shoulder of a fellow hiker and sobbed. Those around the fire supported him with compassion. As he dried his eyes, the eighteen-year-old said, "When my life was spared, I knew at a gut level that I was saved for a reason—that I had a purpose for being on this planet. I had to get well so I could find that purpose. I now know my Mission of Service is to create a healthy planet by healing the sick."

That mission became Nicholas's guiding light. He devoted himself to his own healing and the healing of others. Eight years later, he graduated from medical school and began his career as a physician. He sent Rick a note of gratitude for his life-changing experience around the campfire in Wisconsin. He wrote, "Little did I know that my health crisis as a teenager would lead me to a dream career as a doctor healing people's wounds. I am now living my mission."

For some, the word *intention* means focusing on getting the right house, career, car, bank account, and partner. That form of intention can be ego-driven with the accumulation of objects as the prime objective. Success then becomes defined as attracting the right stuff.

Our intention is to help men discover the Power Tool of purpose and meaning in their lives. From that place, they consciously create a mission to utilize their knowledge, talents, and skills to be of service. The word *mission* has long been discussed in corporate and business circles. Many corporations have mission statements displayed in their foyer. While they profess accountability to the statement, they often pay scant attention to the real power of mission in the lives of their employees.

Mission is central to men living fully in the world as awakened men, as well as helping men make a lasting positive impact on others. It shines directly from our souls, informed by our wounds and our talents. We may not yet be fully aware of our mission or have the message clear in our hearts and souls; however, many of us sense there's a purpose to our existence and that we have something profound to offer the world.

Discovering a mission of service is a transpersonal process that invites conscious connection with our inner Spirit, Higher Power, or whatever we call that which is greater than ourselves. From that place, we recognize our purpose, align our lives, and embrace the call to help change the world. Armed with a clear intention to follow our mission, we utilize that Power Tool to leave a legacy that services the world.

Mission is essentially combining our vision or purpose with action. This can be simply stated in the equation: **Vision + Action = Mission of Service.**

POWER TOOL OF VISION

While vision can emerge from an innate passion or talent, powerful visions come from our inner boy's wounds. The paradox is that out of our deepest wounds come our greatest gifts. Wounds can make us experts at understanding what we so desperately needed. Therefore, our vision is often an attempt to heal childhood wounds and give to the world what we most needed. Who is more motivated to learn about peace than the person who experienced constant chaos in his early life? Who better to urge the world to find love than a person who did not experience that as a child but gained it later as an adult?

To access the Power Tool of vision, we can ask ourselves the following questions:

- What did I not get as a child that I desperately wanted or needed? (Examples: unconditional love, attention from a parent, safety, security, etc.)

- What wounds did I experience? (Examples: lack of fathering, neglect or abandonment, abuse, etc.)

- What am I called to change about myself and the world? (Examples: self-care, accountability, developing a spiritual life, etc.)

- Where does the world need healing? (Examples: churches, education, the environment, government, etc.)

- What values are dear to my heart? (Examples: integrity, honesty, compassion, generosity, etc.)

- How can I be of service? (Examples: volunteering, joining an organization, sharing talents and services, etc.)

RICK

My want for loving parents who freely expressed their love to me and each other was incredibly powerful. My desire for peace in a household beset by chaos, separation, and fear was palpable. My vision was to bring about the very things in others what I had most wanted but did not get as a child.

As a result, early in life, I felt a sense of responsibility and compassion to make the world a better place. I spent many years of volunteer church work and ten years of service as a Big Brother. However, I had not unearthed the wounds that needed healing or owned my capacity to serve and change the world.

LEONARD

Growing up, I felt anxious and insecure in a home that did not feel safe. I survived by becoming invisible so that I wouldn't get attacked verbally or emotionally. I didn't talk to anyone about the painful wounds that I felt as a child. Those wounds propelled me on a quest to find my voice, express my truth, and create an inner loving home.

The ancient quest for the Philosopher's Stone was really a quest to turn the lead of our wounds into the gold of a Mission of Service. The alchemists of the Middle Ages were looking for a way to transform the lead weight of our pain into the gold of our gifts, as expressed through our mission. An awareness of our purpose energizes us and gives us a reason to stay engaged and live fully.

Dr. Martin Luther King, Jr. turned the wounds of racial discrimination into a vision for the world that he eloquently stated in his "I Have a Dream" speech. Norman Vincent Peale overcame his own negativity by promoting the Power of Positive Thinking. Nelson Mandela turned the ugliness of Apartheid into freedom.

POWER TOOL OF ACTION

Vision without action is a daydream. Action without vision is a nightmare.

—*Japanese Proverb.*

A vision without action leads nowhere. Action without a clear vision makes it ineffective or even downright dangerous. When we join vision with action, we form an unstoppable force to transform the world. As we hold a grand vision, we employ action to make that vision a reality.

Organizations and people who are driven by a mission with a clearly stated vision supported by potent actions stand out in the world. Consider these extra-ordinary individuals:

- Dr. King did not just dream. He marched with his followers, faced abuse, and eventually paid the ultimate price for his leadership.

- Mother Theresa did not just talk about serving the poorest and neediest in India. She worked in the streets, humbly lifting untouchables out of the gutter and lovingly administering to them.

- Harvey Milk championed gay rights as the first openly gay elected official in California and was assassinated.

- Malala Yousafzai overcame an assassination attempt by the Taliban to promote education for women.

- Sadiq Khan, the first Muslim mayor of London, promoted tolerance and unity.

- Chris Long, the Philadelphia Eagles defensive lineman, donated his 2017 base salary of $1 million to help underserved youth in the three NFL cities where he played.

These individuals became shining examples of people of mission who helped to transform the world. **They didn't just talk about their visions; they lived them every day!**

If we are not committed to being of service, we can detour into wrong action which is ego-driven and self-serving. Right action takes us steadily up the proverbial mountain toward our mission. That may involve taking courses, learning leadership skills, attending men's groups, or finding a coach. Those actions can further the unique talents or gifts we can use to manifest our vision. In the beginning of this chapter, we described the path of Nicholas. He took action by studying medicine so that he could serve his vision of healing.

Consider these questions to uncover the Power Tool of action:

- Name your passion, talent, or gifts. (For example, music, art, writing, teaching, coaching, building, renovating, learning, etc.)

- What talent or gift have you wanted to develop? (For example, learning to play the guitar, going back to school, becoming certified as a coach, joining the Peace Corps, etc.)

- What will you give back to the world?

- What steps can you take now to actualize your vision?

CREATE YOUR MISSION OF SERVICE

Never doubt that a small group of thoughtful, committed, citizens can change the world. Indeed, it is the only thing that ever has.

— Margaret Meade

Samurais of Japan live by a code of behavior called *Bushido* that encompasses principles, purpose, and mission. You are now ready to create your own code or Mission of Service by combining your vision with action. Together, they become a super Power Tool. Remember, Vision + Action = Mission of Service.

- Who do you know or admire who lives a mission to bring about change?

- What is your *bushido*? What do you hold sacred?

- What are you willing to truly live for?

- What are you willing to die for?

- What action can you take?

145

🐾 LEONARD

My initial mission had to do with healing wounded souls through my words and actions—a good fit whenever I conducted therapy. However, as I began to write and speak, I was called to upgrade my mission statement to the following: I connect with Spirit and use my words to inspire others to return home to love and inner peace. That has become my guiding light.

🐾 RICK

My mission statement came to me like an epiphany in a circle of fifty men on the Saturday morning of my New Warrior Training Adventure back in 1990. My Mission of Service is to create a passionately loving and peaceful planet by speaking, writing, and leading safe, sacred, diverse healing circles.

OTHER EXAMPLES OF MISSION OF SERVICE

- Create a stimulating educational environment and teach children the principles of living holistically.

- Produce a healed world by healing myself and others.

- Build a loving planet by loving myself and others.

- Create healthy and loved animals by healing them as a veterinarian.

- Construct sustainable and welcoming environments by designing beautiful and functional buildings.

- Protect and serve my country by serving in the armed forces.

Our Mission of Service defines our life's work. It gives us a reason to leap out of bed in the morning and serve passionately. It guides our lives in directions that help us stay energized and effective. Our mission can direct us to establish a new career, write a book, change locations, alter relationships, or mentor others. It can change over time, depending on what mountains we are called to climb. However, the core values embedded in the vision, such as promoting healing, unity, love, etc., usually remain the same.

WHAT STOPS US FROM LIVING A MISSION OF SERVICE?

Our shadows, or unconscious parts of ourselves, can prevent us from recognizing our mission. Harkening back to our earlier discussion of shadows, remember that both dark and golden aspects of ourselves hide in shadows. Therefore, in addition to a Golden Mission, we also have a Dark Mission. The *Star Wars* movies represented these two aspects as the *Force* and the *Dark Side*.

While our Missions of Service represents our inner gold, we must be aware that our Dark Mission can operate in the background even if we are unaware of it. In fact, for many of us, our Dark Mission operates as our default setting operating silently until we activate our Mission of Service. Our work is to uncover and bring to light both these energies and tendencies through our own personal shadow mining.

RICK

While doing my shadow mining, I discovered that my Dark Mission was to create a hateful planet of isolation by withholding all I have to offer and shaming what others had to offer. That was virtually the mirror image of my Mission of Service where a soulful, tender, and powerful part of myself yearned to give back something of value to the world. I can now clearly glimpse my capacity to harm myself and others when I express my Dark Mission. I have worked hard at recognizing these two missions and incorporating an awareness of their influence into my daily practice so that I can evaluate how well I am living my Mission of Service.

LEONARD

When I fall back into the shadows of insecurity, unworthiness, unlovability, or not feeling good enough, I move away from the eight dimensions and disconnect from Spirit. My Dark Mission then becomes ego-driven to feel better than others by using my words to criticize others and see them as inadequate so that I can feel more adequate.

When I judge others as being small and inflate myself as being more important, I am operating out of my Dark Mission. If I catch myself stepping into that shadow, I try to wake up so I can show up with my Mission of Service.

OTHER EXAMPLES OF DARK MISSIONS

- Hating losing and losers, so I am here to win at all costs, even if it means destroying my competition.

- Advocating white supremacy and abhorring diversity by working to ensure that white males hold privilege.

- Creating pain and chaos by diving into my addictions.

- Avoiding responsibility by blaming others for everything that is wrong.

- Isolating by withholding my feelings and thoughts from those whom I love.

Another way that we stop ourselves from living our mission is by letting our *shoulds* dictate our lives. These are the messages that caregivers and institutions have given us about how we should think, feel, and behave. We may be imprisoned by golden handcuffs to an unfulfilling job that provides financial security yet offers little emotional reward.

When we follow the *shoulds* of others, we lose contact with our innate truth. Doing so, we end up living as Oscar Wilde once stated, "Most people are other people. Their thoughts are some-one else's opinions, their lives a mimicry, their passion a quotation." Adhering to a Mission of Service shuts out those *should* messages and focuses on what is true and important for us. In other words, we stop "shoulding" on ourselves!

USING A MISSION STATEMENT TO POWER THROUGH PROBLEMS

Whenever we are confronted with a problem that requires a decision, we can ask these questions:

- Is this decision aligned with my mission?

- Will this opportunity allow me to intentionally manifest my vision or will it take me away from it?

- Will this activity help me foster my purpose in the world?

- Can I radiate my mission in this setting?

If the answer to these questions is *no*, what stops you from saying, "No, thanks"? If the answer is *yes*, then you can joyfully throw your energy, expertise, exuberance, and passion into the project, knowing that your soul will be fed even as you serve others.

Our mission is a powerful touchstone to gauge how we live each day. If in alignment, the day was probably well spent and fulfilling. It may have been challenging, but our action would have been purpose driven. If our day was not in alignment with mission, we would sense that we missed some golden opportunities to impact the lives around us. We may have settled for selfishness, laziness, or passed up a chance to serve a friend or cause. Maybe we gave in to anger, fear, or harshly judged a loved one. Perhaps, we became unconscious of the impact of our behavior on others.

When you leave behind those activities that don't align with your mission, you will use your time and energy powerfully and with purpose. You will recognize when you act out of service and when you act out of sacrifice. The former will fill and sustain you while the latter will drain and deplete you. Your mission-driven activities will generate joy and fulfillment, and you will experience energy that floods your heart and soul.

Before you go to bed, reflect on the activities of the day. If you were out of alignment, learn from that experience. You can then create an intention to redirect your thoughts and behaviors for the upcoming day. Stating your Mission of Service shortly after you wake up will remind you to make choices congruent with your vision and power up your life.

HENRY

Henry, one of Rick's dearest friends, has been in a men's group for thirty-two years. He created a powerful Mission of Service: "By Divine grace and God's love, I create a global village of diversity and inclusion." When he was in his late thirties, Henry decided that one way for him to fully live his mission was to establish a program to work with young people of color, many of whom were headed for trouble as gangbangers. He wrote up a proposal and submitted it to the State of Wisconsin Department of Public Instruction and was granted $60,000 to implement what he named "The PRIDE Program."

Along with other colleagues he enlisted, Henry leveraged this grant into a program that ran for ten years in schools in Kenosha, Wisconsin. His mission was so compelling and authentic that he attracted many men and women to serve in his program. In the process, he touched the lives of countless high-school-aged Black and Latino boys and girls. Gangbangers and longtime enemies agreed to put away their colors to do this life-changing work together. They opened their hearts and discovered their own Missions of Service, thus changing the trajectories of their lives.

To this day, many of the PRIDE graduates keep track of Henry and his team through social media as they complete college and start careers that serve others. Teachers, ministers, and social workers were born out of the PRIDE Program. These men and women of color make no bones about the positive influence that Henry and the PRIDE Program have had on their lives. Because of his Mission of Service, Henry created a powerful community that changed individual lives.

THE POWER TOOL OF INTENTION

Making our Mission a reality often requires us to manifest specific goals like having sufficient finances, promoting a vision, building a business, or creating an audience. Therefore, we must identify and clarify our intentions to manifest them in the material world. The following diagram of a flower with six petals takes us through the Power Tool of Intention, a six-stage process that takes us Home with our Mission complete.

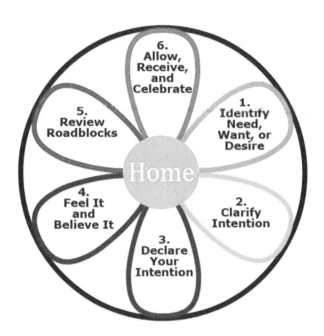

STAGE 1. IDENTIFY NEED, WANT, OR DESIRE

Becoming intentional starts with unearthing a need, want, or desire, not always an easy process. Since many of us have been taught as children to suppress our needs and desires, we may have difficulty identifying basic ones such as attaining self-esteem, exercising personal power, connecting with others, having our voice heard and recognized, and living a purposeful life.

At times, we may know what we want but are unclear about our underlying needs. If this is the case, we can become archeologists and dig beneath the surface by asking, "What do I really need, want, or desire in this situation?" Asking that question can help us discover what is truly important. Our answer will lead us to consciously use the power of intention to satisfy an unmet need or fulfill a heart's desire.

🎭 RICK AND LEONARD

Both of us had a desire to share our knowledge and our years of experience working with men. Our initial intention was to write a book together. That seemed simple enough since we both had written several books. However, as we identified our desire, we stepped onto the six-stage process that evolved into a life of its own. Our desire to help men expanded beyond one book to several and now includes webinars and presentations.

STAGE 2. CLARIFY INTENTION

Once we bring an intention into the light, we must clarify it. Clarification shows us what we clearly want as well as what we do not want. Both sharpen the image of our ultimate goal. This very process may raise conflicting beliefs. For example, if we want to have sufficient money to create a not-for-profit business to build wells in an impoverished country but have an embedded belief about poverty, we will encounter resistance when money comes our way.

A conflicting belief reduces the impact of an intention. Shadows obscure the light, so uncovering our shadow beliefs raises our awareness and crystallizes our intention to fulfill a desired goal. Often, we need money, passion, connection, relationships, and resources. However, we may also need inner healing, love, perseverance, focus, and guidance to sustain us along the journey.

🎭 LEONARD AND RICK

As we clarified our intention to write a book, we spent considerable time together to identify our audience and what we wanted to say to them. We also had to clarify who was going to do what and when we would do it. As well, we had to come up with a marketing plan on how to get our book into the world. What became evident was that neither of us enjoys marketing. Our passion centers around writing, teaching, and coaching, not selling. Therefore, we knew we would have to face our reluctance to promote ourselves. That surfaced an underlying shadow belief of not being good enough that required deeper healing.

STAGE 3. DECLARE YOUR INTENTION

Declaring an intention is, by itself, an act of creation. We give our desire a powerful voice and start a chain reaction with empowered words that paint an image of a desired outcome. If we were encouraged as children to openly express our needs, stating the intention will come easy. However, if we were taught to suppress our voice, then this step will be more challenging.

In men's work, we often use declarations, particularly to counteract any negative belief we were taught while growing up. Declarations set in motion the law of cause and effect because a declaration becomes a verbal reminder of an intention. The *Declaration of Independence* is a great example of an intention that birthed a country.

If you feel uneasy about such a grand intention, you may need to grow into it until it becomes you. And stating a declaration once is not enough. Repeating it constantly anchors it in your subconscious. Writing the declaration down and reading it twice daily, preferably after you wake up and before you retire for the night, will anchor it in your subconscious to grow and expand toward success.

🌀 RICK AND LEONARD

Declaring our intention took us on an interesting journey. Originally, we named our book, "A New Manifesto." However, as we declared our intention to others, we received feedback to come up with a better name. After researching the title with other men and women, we came up with a second title, "Wake Up, Grow Up, and Show Up: Calling Men into the 21st Century." However, the book seemed to have a life of its own. It eventually declared a name, "Power Tools for Men: A Blueprint for Men's Evolution." That declaration led to a website, logo, webinars, Facebook page, and presentations.

STAGE 4. FEEL IT AND BELIEVE IT

In Wayne Dyer's book *You'll See It When You Believe It*, he highlights the power of belief. Beliefs form an internal vision of the world so that what we see on the outside becomes a reflection of our beliefs. If we believe life is a struggle, we will see struggle all around us. If we believe in scarcity, that is what we will notice in the world.

When we couple our beliefs with feelings, we establish a potent force. Emotion is the energy that moves us to action. When we passionately change our beliefs and alter the internal images in our mind, we produced a chain reaction that shapes the outward world.

Elite athletes use the power of intention to actively imagine success by visualizing the feelings associated with peak performances. Phil Jackson, who successfully coached the Chicago Bulls to six championships and then the Los Angeles Lakers to five championships, wrote, "Visualization is the bridge I use to link the grand vision of the team I conjure up every summer to the evolving reality on the court."[44]

🔧 LEONARD AND RICK

We spent countless hours talking about our vision about masculinity. We both believe in the importance of men shifting from the old patriarchal model of manhood and embracing a model where men value emotions and relationships, share with an open heart, relate

---

44   Jackson, Phil and Delehanty, Hugh, *Sacred Hoops: Spiritual Lessons of a Hardwood Warrior*, Hyperion, New York, 1995, P. 121.

authentically, deepen their connection with a Higher Power, embrace a healthy sexual life, live with integrity and intention in community, and access inner Sovereign/King energy. We actively reinforce those beliefs and feelings in ourselves and support other men on their journey to identify and embrace the beliefs and emotions that help them build a better life.

STAGE 5. REVIEW ROADBLOCKS

The Power Tool of Intention is a creative process that often involves roadblocks. If we want to be a professional athlete, obtain a college degree, write a bestseller, build a not-for-profit business, or create a healthy, vibrant community, we will encounter periodic roadblocks over the passage of time. Some intentions take years to complete.

Roadblocks stop us in our tracks so we can shine the light of awareness on our lives and review where we are heading. We may have one or more realizations:

- We are traveling in the wrong direction.

- We need a rest.

- We must take a detour.

- We must dig through negative shadows.

- We need help and require a guide.

Roadblocks always appear for a reason. As we raise our awareness, we find clarity about the next course of action.

🐾 RICK AND LEONARD

While working on this book over the past four years, we have encountered numerous roadblocks. We had to change titles, learn about producing podcasts and webinars, experience rejection from

156

publishers, navigate our relationship so that we did not step on each other's toes, and resolve conflict when it arose. The roadblocks made us take detours such as renaming the book, seeking help from consultants, facing our shadows about not being good enough, and taking time to pause and rest.

STAGE 6. ALLOW, RECEIVE, AND CELEBRATE

Once we've uncovered our needs, clarified an intention, declared it, felt it, believed it, and reviewed any roadblocks, we are ready for the final stage. Now we can allow our desires to manifest, receive them with gratitude, and celebrate our success.

The concept of allowing gives us permission to project outward. Allowing requires that we continually shift our thinking to the uplifting emotional states we wish to experience. If we desire a job where we help others, we must allow anything that moves us in that direction. If we seek financial prosperity, we thankfully welcome each small coin that drops into our lap. If we ask for love, we notice every passing smile and smile back with loving appreciation.

Having a receptive attitude is essential. If we have difficulty receiving, we will push away a cornucopia of blessings. Therefore, we must continually look for evidence that the power tool of intention is doing its job. Every thankful step, small though it may be, reduces the distance between an intention and the desired outcome. Many such steps lead to peak experiences. Along the way, we expand our trust, self-confidence, and personal power.

Celebrations are not saved for the end. Many small victories lead to major ones. The same is true for celebrations. Each time you reward yourself in this unfolding process, you reinforce the fact that you are consciously moving toward your intended goal. Therefore, celebrate often and with others.

♔ LEONARD AND RICK

Like most men, we tend to be action-oriented men who love to fix problems. One of the challenges for us was to allow the book to unfold without forcing it. That also meant we had to allow each other to have his individual voice as well as develop one voice as co-authors. We had to give and receive feedback to one another whenever one of us wrote a section of the book, and we had to receive guidance from those whom we asked for help. We would celebrate each other's achievements and treat ourselves to meals after some accomplishments like completing a draft of the book. We look forward to many more celebrations!

An African proverb says, "If you want to go fast, go alone. If you want to go far, go together." Armed with the Power Tool of Intention as well as the Power Tools of Vision and Action, you now go toward **Community**, the seventh dimension in the CLASSICS model.

INTENTIONALLY STRETCH YOUR VISION INTO A MISSION OF SERVICE

Take some time and meditate on your *vision* of how you want the world to be. How would that world look, smell, taste, and feel? Write or draw your vision of this world.

1. What special talents, knowledge, or gifts do you have that could further your vision if you did it regularly? This *action* may be something you have fantasized about doing such as taking classes or volunteering. Write about doing that action, or, alternately, draw a picture. Notice how that clarifies your action.

2. Join your *vision* with *action* to craft your Mission of Service. How does this statement feel to you? If the Mission of Service feels huge, exciting, and challenging, then it is probably the one for you! If not, keep digging for a unique vision and action that best captures why you are on the planet.

3. Write about how you could employ your mission to serve yourself and others.

4. Create your Dark Mission by writing the exact opposite of what you stated as your Mission of Service. Make sure your Dark Mission has a clear vision and an action. How do you feel when you say your Dark Mission?

5. Share your Mission of Service and your Dark Mission with a loved one and ask them for feedback.

6. Identify a need, want, or desire that helps you fulfill your mission.

7. Clarify an intention that fulfills that need, want, or desire.

8. Declare the intention.

9. Visualize the result by feeling and believing it.

10. Review any roadblocks that might impede your progress.

11. How can you practice allowing, receiving, and celebrating?

Chapter Nine

Build a Life with Community

Communication leads to community, that is, to understanding, intimacy, and mutual valuing.

— *Rollo May*

 RICK

In December 1991, the day after Christmas, my beloved father suddenly died of heart failure when he was just sixty-five-years old. The previous day, I had exercised with him in the morning and then celebrated Christmas at his house with my entire twenty-five-person family. Later, he showed me the plane tickets he had purchased to travel to Greece, one of his lifelong goals. Twenty-four hours later, he was gone, seemingly in an instant.

I was overcome by feelings of loss and grief. It didn't make any sense that my father would have only a few months of retirement after working hard most of his life. Thank God I was learning about not stuffing my feelings. As I sank deeply into my grief, I knew I needed support and became overwhelmed. I did something that would have been impossible two years before—I reached out to my men's group for support.

The next day five loving and open-hearted men appeared at my door. After we sat in a circle, they listened attentively as I shared memories of my wonderful father: he'd never abandoned me even though his relationship with my mother was fraught with years of pain and struggle, he often told me and my siblings how proud he was of us, and he trusted me with intimate details of his life.

As the circle prompted me to tell more about my father, something amazing happened. My friends leaned in and put their arms around me. I fell into their laps and erupted into soul-cleansing sobbing. Snot ran down my chin, and hot tears washed my face, as these men held me lovingly. My grief came like ocean waves crashing, again and again, on my soul's dry and sandy shore.

Though this happened thirty-two years ago, I still see the loving eyes of my friends who unconditionally supported me. Their empathy and support brought a magical, healing moment in my life. I could not have reached this sweet space without the incredible support of this community of men. In moments of loss and stress, there's little more valuable than community support. I repay this gift often by offering my arms to my dear friends who experience loss.

A fabulous Power Tool is to build community with other men. Building community is the seventh tool in our CLASSICS Model. This dynamic contrasts with the old model of isolation. Sadly, men have learned to deny their legitimate emotions and most of the benefits of long-lasting, fulfilling friendships and community.

Daniel Levinson writes in *The Seasons of a Man's Life*, "Close friendship with a man or woman is rarely experienced by American men... In general, most men do not have an intimate friend of the kind they recall fondly from boyhood or youth."[45]

When Leonard conducts an assessment session in therapy, he asks clients about their social network and friendships. Men

---

45   Levinson, Samuel, *The Seasons of a Man's Life*, Knopf, New York, 1973, p. 335.

frequently say they have a few friends or a couple of close friends. However, when asked how often they get together or whether they share personal problems or emotions, their replies reveal that they have few friends, apart from a partner, to whom they expose their true feelings. They could be in the throes of divorce or having serious health issues and still hide their pain. And if a man forms important relationships at work and then changes jobs or retires, he often leaves those relationships behind.

Antwone, a sixty-five-year-old retired engineer, lost his wife of forty years. He sought therapy to deal with his overwhelming grief. Since his wife had organized the social calendar and brought people together for parties, he spent little time developing one-on-one friendships with other men. Except for casual relationships with neighbors and people at his church, he had no friends. When Leonard explored the prospects of a grief group or men's circles, Antwone froze, as if he had been told to jump off a bridge. He nervously asked, "How do I go about making friends?" Answering that question became an important part of his work.

In his book, *The Transparent Self*, Sidney Jourard writes, "Research has shown that men typically reveal less personal information about themselves to others than women [do]. Since men, doubtless, have as much inner experience as women [do], then it follows that men have more secrets from the interpersonal world than women.... Moreover, if a man has something to hide, it must follow that other people will be a threat to him: they might pry into his secrets, or he may, in an unguarded moment, reveal his true self in its nakedness, thereby exposing his areas of weakness and vulnerability."[46]

Isolating ourselves stunts our growth and development. As a consequence, we develop a false self to adapt and connect, thereby reinforcing a disconnection from our authentic self. To present a

---

46 Jourard, Sidney, *The Transparent Self*, Van Nostrand Reinhold Inc., New York, 1971, p. 35.

face of success to the world, we may adopt a conspiracy of silence about pain or trauma, neglect or shame. This silent barrier stops us from reaping the benefits of having someone truly see us. Isolation breeds misery; community offers a sense of belonging.

The educator and motivational speaker, John Bradshaw, echoes this benefit: "In order to be healed, we must come out of hiding and isolation. This means finding a person, or ideally a group of significant others, whom we are willing to trust."[47] He says the only way to find out if we're wrong is to expose ourselves to someone else's scrutiny. "When we trust someone else and experience their love and acceptance, we begin to change our beliefs about ourselves. We learn that we are not bad; we learn that we are loveable and acceptable."[48]

One of the difficulties in sharing feelings is our fear of being seen as effeminate or homosexual. As a result, men stop themselves from opening up to each other. Many men would rather die than expose their feelings to other men! As Sam Keen writes in *Fire in the Belly*, "'Normal' American men are homophobic, afraid of close friendships with other men. The moment we begin to feel warmly toward another man, the 'homosexual' panic button gets pressed.... A predictable result of our homophobia is that men become overdependent on women to fulfill their need for intimacy, and swallow the romantic myth hook, line, and sinker."[49]

The CLASSICS Model of Power Tools advocates that men connect with other men on an ongoing basis to build a sense of brotherhood. Friendships, regardless of their context, have to be developed, no different from developing a skill like golf or tennis. We may feel comfortable fishing or having a beer with buddies but

---

47 Bradshaw, John, *Healing the Shame That Binds You*, HCI Books, Deerfield Beach, FL, 2005, p. 153.

48 Ibid.

49 Keen, Sam, *Fire in the Belly*, Bantam Books, New York, 1991, pp. 174-175.

getting together to deepen a friendship requires intention and commitment to meet regularly and keep in touch, whether in person or by phone or text. Going it alone no longer works. The lonely heroic figures like Rambo or the Lone Ranger from Leonard and Rick's generation did not support healthy, vibrant, thriving men.

We are called to develop male friendships where we establish trust, listen attentively, help each other through the rough spots, offer insights and support, and care for one another. We can clarify our needs and wants and increase our capacity for empathy, love, and connection. It is a rare gift to authentically speak our truth, be seen and heard, and truly see and hear another brother. When we share something personal, we break out of our isolation.

We, Leonard and Rick, have benefitted from support communities throughout our lives and have often heard the remark, "I thought I was the only one who felt that way." Over the years, Rick has participated in a church community, an Adult Child of Dysfunctional Families group, men's groups, breathwork healing circles, and Al-Anon Twelve-Step work. Leonard has benefited from shamanic drumming circles, dream groups, personal development groups, consciousness expanding spiritual communities, and, of course, men's groups.

🔘 LEONARD

When I was a boy, I loved sitting in a circle around a campfire when I went camping with the Boy Scouts. After a day of adventures, we'd gather wood and build a fire. Then we'd sit on logs and watch the sparks dance into the sky. We'd tell jokes, sing songs, and share stories. That feeling of belonging and connection to a group disappeared when I became an adult.

It wasn't until I was thirty-seven years old that I again found a circle of males. They breathed fire back into my belly and awakened my heart and soul. Though I was married with two children, I had felt something was missing. I needed a band of brothers. When I joined the men's group in Sydney, it was as if I had returned to sitting with buddies around the campfire. That first group in Australia opened my heart and soul and fed my passion for writing. Since my wife thought writing was a waste of my time, I soaked in their encouragement and support. Their love stoked my fire to become a writer. I doubt that I would have persevered in writing if it weren't for those men.

Many years later in Chicago, I went through a tortuous divorce after twenty-six years of marriage. I found another circle of men to which I bonded over a seventeen-year period. At my lowest point, facing the pain of separation and divorce, I leaned into the comforting arms of my brothers. I learned that real men grieve. Real men love and comfort one another. And that's what we did whenever any of us faced a crisis or challenge. We brought our problems to the group so that we could be accepted, loved, and cared for. We faced any shame together. Acceptance and love were the norm as we sat in circle, as if around a campfire, watching our sparks dance into the sky.

We acknowledge that taking a leap into authentic male friendships and men's circles can be daunting. We both felt terror some thirty-five years ago when we were first called to climb the mountain toward healthy relationships with men, but we did it anyway. We are grateful for the friendships, love, and support we have received. We use a simple process to connect authentically with another man or a group of men. Consider it a Power Tool to *Check In* with others.

POWER TOOL OF CHECKING IN

- Check In with your feelings. This means going beyond *good* or *fine*. Being Authentic is essential to this process.

- Share what's truly going on in your life. The deeper you share, the more intimate your connection.

- Listen carefully to your partner or partners as they check in.

- Avoid fixing. Just listen, unless you are specifically asked for feedback or suggestions.

- Ask for what you need from the relationship(s) and the group.

Seeking, finding, and giving support regularly are requisite for men to thrive today, an antidote to our natural tendency to isolate. Circles can provide ongoing loving support, accountability, shadow awareness, and growth. By regularly participating in a safe environment, we become aware of each man's personal stories, including his wounds, weaknesses, gifts, and innate magnificence. At the same time, we can call each other on our bullshit, point out shadows, both dark and gold, and hold each other close through personal trauma, loss, or other challenges, while celebrating one another's triumphs and victories. This is a huge payoff to building community!

Be strong, be fearless, be beautiful. And believe that anything is possible when you have the right people there to support you.

— Misty Copeland

Both of us look forward to attending our weekly meetings. Different men step into the role of leader (or King) who provides the group with a personal growth process, for example working on accountability or integrating masculine archetypes. Because we never know what will happen, every meeting becomes an adventure. We're never bored. Most often, we leave the meeting with a growing love and respect and deeper connection for everyone in the community.

Explicit agreements create a safe and supportive environment. We reiterate the rules whenever a new person enters the circle to ensure group safety.

KEY GROUP AGREEMENTS

1. **Confidentiality:** Anything said in the circle that is of a personal nature stays in the circle. Men may share their own work or lessons learned, but not that of another, without permission.

2. **"I" Statements:** True sharing occurs in the first person and requires a self-focus. We use "I" statements, not "You" statements, thereby owning our truth.

3. **Non-Judgmental Attitude:** We avoid contradicting, correcting, or admonishing a man for the way he feels or believes.

4. **No Voyeurs:** We come to the group to do our own work. No one comes just to observe or stay silent. We are all required to participate so we can grow and learn.

5. **Don't Monopolize:** We allow each man to express himself without interruption and avoid monopolizing the conversation.

6. **Giving Feedback:** The most useful feedback is sharing personal feelings and reactions. For example, "When I heard you say...., I felt..." We avoid unsolicited advice or fixing, unless specifically asked for. However, we offer constructive feedback when invited.

The group may add or subtract additional agreements as needed. Sometimes, for example, a group may create a simple ritual for adding a new member or for saying goodbye to men who leave the group so that proper closure occurs between individuals. We want to highlight that most support groups are not therapy groups run by a trained professional. Men who are suicidal, homicidal, or debilitated by mental illness need the help of a therapist. Other men who are unable to respect boundaries and follow agreements aren't suitable participants in a group. On the rare occasion when a member continually disrupts meetings or does not function within the parameters of the group, it may be necessary to dis-invite him. Maintaining and strengthening boundaries builds relationships between members and is vital for a safe and healthy group.

In *Fire in the Belly*, Sam Keen writes, "We need same sex friends because there are types of validation and acceptance that we receive only from our gender mates. There is much about our experience as men that can only be shared with, and understood by, other men. There are stories we can tell only to those who have wrestled in the dark with the same demons and been wounded by the same angels. Only men understand the secret fears that go with the territory of masculinity."[50]

Often, long-term relationships develop as isolated men become transformed by the power of community. A number of men's organizations provide personal development programs, training, and groups, such as the ones we've participated in—ManKind Project and Victories for Men. (Check resources at the back of the book for others.) Many churches now sponsor men's groups that may or may not be faith based.

We want to take the notion of male community a step further. As Bill Kauth writes in *A Circle of Men: The Original Manual for Men's Support Groups*, "A man who is getting healthier and stronger will want to be involved in some larger way, channeling his energy

---

50   Keen, Sam, *Fire in the Belly*, Bantam Books, New York, 1991, pp. 174-175.

into something beyond himself. He may start close to home with his family, then move out into the community and the world."[51] It is a powerful action to work together, as a men's community, to serve the world and our Missions collectively! By doing so, we may find real friendships with men in our group.

POWER TOOL: BUILDING FRIENDSHIPS

As was stated previously, men rarely experience deep, true friendship with other men. Yet doing so is a Power Tool for happiness, connection and even health. How can we build authentic friendships? Here are some strategies we recommend:

1. Make a commitment to reach out and build friendships.

2. Ask about your friends' lives and actively listen.

3. Openly communicate about your life and practice being vulnerable.

4. Show affection and caring with genuine praise.

5. Work through any barriers to intimacy (such as our father issues and betrayals by other men).

🌣 LEONARD

Like most men, I learned to further my career, achieve goals, and get paid for a job well done. Friendships came and went depending on where I worked. When I worked at another job, I built relationships

---

51   Kauth, Bill, *A Circle of Men: The Original Manual for Men's Support Groups*, St. Martin's Press, New York, 1992, p. 85.

based on working together. Now I had a fishing buddy, but our mission was to catch fish, not develop a friendship.

It was not until I became involved in men's work that I realized deep male friendships were not dependent on work but had to be nurtured outside of work. Initially, I felt awkward asking a buddy if he wanted to go out for a meal. That would seem quite normal if we had worked at the same place and were having lunch. But calling a friend to see how he was doing or asking if he wanted to go out for a meal required a commitment on my part to build a friendship and a mutual desire from my buddy.

Now I'll call friends on a regular basis to connect. We might chat on the phone or meet up for a meal or walk by the beach. And I make sure to let my friends know that I appreciate them and our relationships.

THE POWER TOOL OF MULTICULTURAL AWARENESS

We tend to gravitate toward individuals and groups that hold similar values, life experiences, and beliefs. These reinforce our world view and a sense of belonging to a particular tribe. The drawback is that other tribes can be viewed as inferior or even threatening, thereby producing distrust or even tribal warfare. Consider the political climate between Democrats and Republicans, the left and the right, for example. Inclusiveness and diversity are huge issues that require a much deeper treatment than we have space for here. Yet, we believe that developing the Power Tool of Multicultural Awareness is crucial to the success of any men's community.

To create more inclusiveness, we must expand our community beyond our familiar neighborhood and step into a broader world that involves a diversity of men and women. Most of us embrace the notion that all men are created equal. Unfortunately, the biases and prejudices that we've picked up from our parents, institutions, and our culture, many of which are unconscious, promote separation versus oneness. That goes against the motto on the Great Seal of the United States, *E pluribus unum* (one out of the many). Divisions in the community occur with racism, sexism, and ageism, and heterosexism, a few of the "isms" that maintain separate tribes.

The Power Tool of Multicultural Awareness calls us to claw our way out of the multicultural morass of unconsciousness and create a wider inclusive community that embraces diversity. If we want to welcome diversity, we need to be aware that our society treats men and women differently based on such characteristics as race, age, gender, religion, sexual orientation, culture, ability, educational level, immigrant status, and so on. Deeply embedded differences in our culture and our psyches impact the lives of men and women in profound ways. For example, we are all aware of the upheaval over racial injustice that has enveloped our country and the world recently since the murder of George Floyd. People of all races have been marching, speaking out, and becoming justice advocates in numbers not seen since the 1960s, demanding much-needed change.

Since our culture is saturated with constant messages about who is more valuable and who is less valuable; who gets a seat at the table, and who doesn't; whose voice is heard, and whose isn't; we must first recognize our unconscious -*isms*. The effects of our different beliefs are often subtle, yet they have a profound impact on how we feel individually as men. They influence whether we interact in ways that are safe, respectful, and accepting. Few of us are willing to admit to personally having biases that are racist, heterosexist, or misogynist. However, our culture influences the way we see the world, injecting us with implicit biases that, if they remain unchallenged, will limit our growth and cause us to not expand our circles beyond our tribe.

When we, Rick and Leonard, were growing up, few black faces were seen on TV. Cowboys were portrayed as heroes and Indians as savages. Men made the money while women stayed at home.

Today's films portray most male superheroes as single. In the 2015 movie, *Avengers: Age of Ultron*, only one superhero, Hawkeye, was a father. He left his pregnant wife and two children so that he could help save the world. The underlying message was that staying at home to look after children was far less heroic than battling powerful enemies.

Our biases are lodged in our psyches and may be invisible until someone points them out, or we unearth them by questioning and challenging the embedded messages from our parents, teachers, churches, media, and culture. We may hold beliefs such as "our country is the best in the world," or "those who practice certain religions are heathens," or "women are not as capable or smart as men."

Warning: it's important not to blame or shame ourselves when we discover our prejudices! We all have them. So, it is incumbent on us to be gentle with ourselves and others as we dig up our biases and oppressions. We can notice and respectfully acknowledge differences between us and others. It is not racist to notice there's a black man in our circle, nor is it homophobic to notice a gay or bisexual man. Becoming aware of our emotional reactions to differences can lead us to change our perspective. Likewise, paying attention to our privileges leads us to greater awareness. This is a lifetime's work! However, together we can root out the beliefs that oppress people, cause separation, and create a diverse community that thrives.

RICK

In 2000 I worked with a group of Australian Aboriginal men in Brisbane using a group process called "The Hero's Journey." Eleven native men, along with eight white Australian men, participated in the circle. One of the men, Monti, who was living on a reservation near Melbourne, stood in the center of the group.

With shoulders hunched over, he kept his eyes on the floor. "My culture has been taken from me," he said. "My people are dying. Our language is dying. My family is dying. I am dying." When asked what he needed, he spoke softly as tears formed in his eyes. "I want to find my culture and restore it. But I don't know how."

When asked to pick a fellow Aborigine to help him, he chose Warrin, a dignified white-haired Aboriginal elder.

Warrin stood tall and faced Monti. "I will help you under one condition. Help me reclaim our culture too, because I am lost as well!"

As the two men identified their own heroic battle to recover their lost heritage, they saw each other as allies on the same journey. They shared the grief and despair of losing their community. Monti reached out and grabbed Warrin. They hugged and released a guttural wail from the depths of their souls. That triggered the other Aborigines to wail an eerie cry that released heartbreaking pain and despair over losing their heritage.

The white men in the circle stood silently shoulder to shoulder as they formed a wall of compassion around these men to contain and honor their grief. Tears flowed like hot lava down each man's face, white and black, as each man witnessed a sacred healing in community.

After what seemed forever, the wailing stopped. Monti looked around the room and proudly announced, "As a man among men, I reclaim my culture and heal my people."

All the men responded in unison, "We hear you!" to reinforce and support Monti's new affirmation. He no longer had to be alone in his grief. He was connected to a community of other heroes to help heal the world.

That story illustrates that healing occurs in diverse men's circle where individuals feel safe and respected. We can't stress enough that men grow and develop through relationships that are critical to our ongoing evolution. As Lionel Tiger writes in his book,

Men in Groups, "The nature of masculinity is for men in groups to empower each other to do what they need to do to ensure the survival of the community. It is imperative that we draw on this evolutionary heritage and bond together globally to respond to our common planetary problems."[52]

We invite men to find and participate in a community, a tribe. True superheroes reach out and connect with other men. They become stewards for home, country, and planet and step into **Sovereignty** as Kings, the final dimension of the CLASSICS Model.

---

52 Tiger, Lionel, *Men in Groups, Third Edition*, Routledge Publishers, New York, 2017.

175

STRETCH INTO COMMUNITY

1. Name your friends and your support group(s).

2. If you're not in a circle, research men's groups that are available in your area and make a plan to attend one. Even better, invite a friend to join you! (NOTE: If you live in a rural area, take heart. Virtual groups offer an alternative.)

3. What have you gained from a community of men?

4. What have you given back to the community?

5. List five issues in your life you'd like to address with one or more supportive men. (No more going it alone!)

6. Which of your above list could be addressed by an ongoing circle of men?

7. Name any biases or prejudices that keep you separate from other men.

8. How can you bring more diversity into your life?

Chapter Ten

Build a Life with Sovereign/King Energy

When we are accessing the King energy correctly, as servants of our own inner King, we will manifest in our own lives the qualities of the good and rightful King, the King in his fullness.

— Robert Moore & Douglas Gillette

The *Game of Thrones*, a popular TV series, deals with kings and their empires. Kings can be tyrants, weaklings, or wise and inspirational. We both had the pleasure of attending workshops and seminars with authors Robert Moore and Doug Gillette in Chicago in the 90s. These two authors have impacted men's work around the world for many years. Their seminal work, *King, Warrior, Magician, Lover: Rediscovering the Archetypes of the Mature Masculine*, presented universal archetypes of men's psyches. They drew upon the work of Swiss psychiatrist Carl Jung who described these archetypes as instinctual patterns and energetic configurations that provide the foundation of our thoughts, feelings, and human behaviors. The archetypes are "… constant and universal in all of us…. These blueprints appear to be great in number, and they manifest themselves as both male and female. There are archetypes that pattern the thoughts and feelings and relationships of women, and there are archetypes that pattern the thoughts and feelings and relationships of men."[53]

Another way of understanding this concept is to realize that all men around the world have similar physical features (two testicles, a nose, two arms, and so forth.) Similarly, men have patterns structured in the psyche that are universal. For example, the warrior archetype is hard-wired, whether in Japan with the Samurai, in Africa with Zulu Warrior, or in Britain with their Marines. All serve to defend and protect the realm. While there are many archetypes, Moore and Gillette's work focused on the four main ones for men.

KING

The authors write, "The King energy is primal in all men.... It comes first in importance, and it underlies and includes the rest of the archetypes in perfect balance. The good and generative King is also a good Warrior, a positive Magician, and a great Lover. And yet, with most of us, the King comes online last."[54] Our Sovereign/ King energy is meant to order and direct our resources and other archetypes, create new life, and bless those who enter our realm.

Since many of us have not been raised in castles with a good, wise King/father figure, we may have slipped into one of the dark shadows of the King, namely being a weakling or a tyrant. On the news we hear countless stories of political figures and businessmen who emulate one or the other. When we lose touch with our authentic inner authority, we create chaos around us. A kingdom without a King has no one to lead.

---

53 Moore, Robert and Gillette, Douglas, *King, Warrior, Magician, Lover: Rediscovering the Archetypes of the Mature Masculine*, HarperCollins, San Francisco, 1990, pp. 10-11.

54 Ibid, p. 49.

We are called to manifest that sovereign energy and stand tall as a healthy King. We are called to lead our families, our workplace, our church, and our organizations—anywhere the need is apparent. With an inner knowing, the King walks with authority, harnesses power, and integrates our psyche's advisors, particularly the Warrior, Magician, and Lover.

Accessing our inner King does not mean that we lord ourselves over others. Rather, we act as a steward. In fact, the balanced King embodies the CLASSICS Model. He is connected to emotions and senses, loves with an open heart, authentically relates to others, and is imbued with Spirit. He channels sexual energy and intentionally propagates a mission in service to the community.

Any King has a scepter that signifies authority and outward power and a crown that symbolizes royalty and inner strength. Harnessing these energies is not easy, for if the King cannot balance these energies, he is prone toward tyranny or helplessness.

Tyrants rule with little regard for others. Narcissistic tyrants seek to dominate. Showing little empathy, they use anger to bully and harass subordinates. They take little or no responsibility for their behavior and blame others for any failures. They rarely shower blessings on others, especially adversaries. However, tyrants favor those who serve them with unquestioned loyalty. Stalin, Hitler, and Saddam Hussein are extreme examples of such Kings.

When a tyrant King rules our lives, we can become tyrants at work, browbeat employees, or emotionally and physically abuse children or partners. We become grandiose and defensive and unable to take critical feedback. Countless movies depict tyrant Kings. In *Gladiator*, Commodus killed his father, Marcus Aurelius, and terrorized those around him. In the *Great Santini*, Robert Duvall played Lieutenant Colonel Wilbur "Bull" Meechum, who treated his family like soldiers who had to adhere to his rules or be subjugated to harassment and abuse. Over time, tyrants end up lonely and forsaken men.

The opposite of the tyrant is the weakling/abdicator who allows fear, shame, and guilt to plague the kingdom. Lacking confidence, discipline, and conviction, he surrenders his inner authority and lets others bully and control him. Anarchy reigns in the weakling's inner and outer kingdom. In the movie *Braveheart*, the king's son is a clear example of the weakling. Dominated by his father, "Longshanks" King Edward, the prince pampers himself and the fawning members of the court during his father's absence. When his father returns, he shrinks in fear, unable to stand up for himself, and abdicates any power.

When we fall into the weakling, we are indecisive at work or home. We squander our time and energy and fail to utilize other energies at our disposal. Fortunately, we can always access the healthy King who is programmed into our psyche. He will send us signs whenever we need direction.

🌀 LEONARD

Many years ago, when I was going through a divorce, I felt powerless and enraged about the end of my marriage of twenty-six years. However, during that time I kept noticing that whenever I drove, signs kept catching my attention—King Carpet, King Car Wash, Martin Luther King Drive, and on and on it went. Then it dawned on me. My healthy King was sending me signs to embrace my sovereign energy and refrain from becoming a weakling or tyrant while divorcing. My mature King stewarded me through the separation by directing me to a good lawyer (Warrior), connecting with a mediator and a therapist (Magician), and receiving encouragement, care, and support from my men's group (Lover). Those forces helped me establish a new life as a single man.

Moore and Gillette state that the Warrior, Magician, and Lover, like the King, are hardwired in us. As the steward, the King directs those energies, and they, in turn, act in service to the King. In the mythological stories such as King Arthur, there are always a

Magician, Warrior, and Lover who help the King maintain balance and direction over the realm.

RICK

During much of my life, I hid my authentic King in shadow. I didn't know how to bless myself or others, nor did I have a sense of my real power. In doing leadership training, I quickly ran up against my wounded, weakling King who had bedeviled me for much of my life. He was unexpressed due to my fear of being abusive, like my mom had been. That fear debilitated me from leading a sacred, kingly life.

On one men's weekend training, I was asked to build a fire and heat the rocks for a sweat lodge. As I stacked logs in the fire pit, one of the men on staff stepped into the pit and kicked down the logs and began rearranging them. Furious, I walked away. In the past, I would have abdicated my sovereign energy by stomping away in anger and avoiding confrontation. I took a few deep breaths and realized that my inner King needed my Warrior to speak, not out of anger or blame, but out of my sovereign energy to protect my realm.

I calmly but forcefully approached the man and asked, "Who is in charge of starting this fire?"

He hesitated a moment, then responded, "Well, you are."

"That's right!" I said, then added, "Did I ask you for help?"

"No."

"Then I ask you to leave my fire alone and let me do my job. I'll ask for help if I need it. Okay?"

Much to my surprise, the man acquiesced and left. Having accessed my King in a healthy way, I returned to the fire pit to complete my work. Sometime later, that man returned to talk. He told me that his father would be attending the training. "I badly wanted him to have a perfect experience. When you set up the fire in a different manner from how I was taught, my fear took over. I was compelled to fix your work. You showed me the impact of my fear. I'm sorry I dissed your work. When you asserted yourself, I knew I could trust you to be straight with me because you wouldn't put up with my bullshit. You helped me trust this container to initiate my dad."

That conversation taught me the importance of stepping into my King and speaking my truth.

QUESTIONS FOR YOUR KING

- How can you create healthy aspects of your kingdom? (Examples: tell your children that you love them, bless your partner or spouse for his/her work and contributions, or notice and celebrate your successes.)

- Who needs your wisdom and support? (Examples: your children, spouse, friends, coworkers, or community.)

- Remember a time when your tyrant or weakling King was in charge. Describe what happened. (Examples: demanded total obedience, made decisions in a vacuum or all alone, were indecisive, or ignored signs that change needed to happen.)

- What story do you carry that disempowers your Kingly energy? (Examples: not feeling good enough, believing you have nothing of value to offer, or worrying your weaknesses will be discovered or exploited.)

- What story do you carry that empowers your Kingly energy? (Examples: you deserve to rule your own life, you are worthy and powerful, or you can access inner advisors.)

Let's now briefly explore the other potent energies in our male psyche that our inner King can draw upon:

LOVER

The **Lover** promotes connection, compassion, cooperation, aliveness, spirituality, romance, and love. He expresses beauty, sensuality, and sexuality. He dissolves boundaries and longs for unity and a sense of meaning to life. "The Lover keeps the other masculine energies humane, loving and related to each other and to the real-life situation of human beings."[55] Artists, musicians, writers, mystics, creatives, and dreamers are those who embody the healthy, balanced Lover.

According to Moore and Gillette when our lover is overexpressed, the addict takes over. Who among us has not felt the siren pull of our addictions for substances, money, love, or power? And an undeveloped lover brings out our impotence. The resulting numbness and lack of aliveness cause us to be withdrawn and even depressed.

If we have become totally immersed in our work and have neglected our emotions, senses, and pleasure, our King can call upon the Lover to make time to enjoy our lives and experience beauty in the world. If we are fearful of intimate relationships, have rigid boundaries, or are forever angry, our King can open our Lover's heart so that we can dissolve into love. The King works with the Lover to provide structure so the energy can be channeled creatively.

John Lennon, a highly generative and creative artist, exemplified the sweet, yet balanced Lover archetype, both in his music and in his life. His love flowed through his music in such songs as "Give Peace a Chance," "Come Together," "Beautiful Boy," and "Oh My Love." To this day Lennon's music continues to touch hearts and souls.

QUESTIONS FOR YOUR LOVER

- Why do you stop yourself from loving? (Examples: fearing that I will be sucked dry from loving fully, giving

---

55   Ibid, p. 140.

more than getting, being subsumed by another, or being rejected or abandoned.)

- What grief has not been expressed that stands in the way of your fully activated Lover? (Examples: father wound, loss of loved ones, previous loss of relationships, or not being loved unconditionally as a child.)

- When in your life have you been addicted or impotent? Describe what happened. (Examples: watching too much TV or porn, drinking too much, being asexual, or fearing intimacy.)

- How can you open your heart to love your kingdom more fully? (Examples: be open and receptive to the love around you, express gratitude to those in your realm such as children and your partner or write a love poem.)

- What needs to begin anew or blossom? (Examples: finding a career you love, seeking a partner or renewing a love relationship, finding a spiritual practice that fuels the soul, or noticing beauty in the world.)

WARRIOR

The Warrior provides power, energy, perseverance, decisiveness, and discipline as he fights through challenges and obstacles. He establishes and defends boundaries for protection and perseveres with courage to complete tasks. Lawyers, police, athletes, and soldiers are jobs that access the Warrior energy. Moore and Gillette speak of the overdeveloped Warrior as the sadist, while the masochist represents an underdeveloped Warrior. The sadist loves to use his power to cause pain or to control others; he is the classic abusive bully. The masochist, however, takes no responsibility for his life, can't defend his boundaries, and likes to play the victim by hurting himself.

Leonard's friend, John Barry, is a fine example of a balanced, clear warrior. A former captain in the US Marine Corps, John served in Vietnam in 1972 and remained in the Corps for twelve years. While he no longer serves in the military, he still adheres to the Marines' motto, *Semper Fi*. Always faithful to the spirit of the Warrior, he describes what being a Marine has taught him. "As a Marine, I developed character and learned discipline and focus. I became part of a company of men who endured hardship together. We were dedicated to work toward a common goal. We never quit, seeking to accomplish our missions, even in the face of life-threatening situations. We had a code: no lying, cheating, or stealing; and we wouldn't tolerate anyone who did any of the above."

There are times when we must call upon our Warrior. If we become addicted, depressed, lethargic, or undisciplined, our King can direct the Warrior to take charge and battle whatever stops us from stepping into the fullness of our lives. We may be asked to set limits with work, establish firm boundaries in a codependent relationship, or stand up for our self when feeling exploited or mistreated. Warriors carry a psychic shield that protects and an imaginary sword that cuts through what no longer serves. The King ensures that our Warrior compassionately fights the good fight.

QUESTIONS FOR YOUR WARRIOR

- What boundaries need to be set or defended? (Examples: dealing with family finances, managing time, or paying attention to self-care.)

- How do you fiercely defend your values? (Examples: knowing what's worth fighting for, standing up for what you believe, or saying a clear "Yes" to that which you want to do and "No" to that which you don't.)

- Describe a time when you avoided owning your power? (Examples: abdicating your responsibility, withholding your truth, or not showing up when needed.)

- What power do you need to move your life forward? (Examples: changing jobs, filing for divorce, creating a more disciplined life, or attending marriage counseling?)

MAGICIAN

The Magician utilizes his mind for introspection, awareness, learning, and communication. He illuminates wisdom and insight to see beyond the material realm. As a master of transformation, technology, and alchemy, he promotes forgiveness and healing. Therapists, doctors, healers, trainers, teachers, scientists, and computer technicians access the Magician energy. Again, according to Gillette and Moore, the naïve innocent (or gullible) one is the underdeveloped Magician, the one who feigns helplessness and ignorance. The detached manipulator, however, represents an overdeveloped Magician, using his intellect and education to overpower, take leadership, and manipulate his followers.

If we lack knowledge or self-awareness, have difficulty communicating with others, or feel disconnected from our mind, body, and spirit, our King can invoke the Magician. We may be guided toward books or self-development programs. We may be called to learn meditation, attend a spiritual center, join a twelve-step program, or see a healer or therapist. Our Magician will teach us about using our mind to heal and manifest our desires. The King directs the Magician to perform his magic with the vision and mission in mind.

Stephen Hawking clearly represents the Magician archetype. Despite suffering tremendous physical challenges from Lou Gehrig's disease (ALS), he persevered to become one of the most creative and productive physicists of our time. He wrote the best-selling book, *A Brief History of Time*, using a painstaking process, one letter at a time with a mouth pointer. Using his mind, he made incredible discoveries about black holes and the origin of the universe.

QUESTIONS FOR YOUR MAGICIAN

- What must be done to access inner knowledge, spiritual understanding, or exceptional magic? (Examples: mediate or pray, delve into studies that serve you, or connect with the mystery and beauty of life.)

- Can you think of a time when your detached manipulator or naïve innocent was in charge? Describe. (Examples: using shame to manipulate, coercing others into doing what you want, pretending to know something you don't actually know, or feigning ignorance to get out of responsibility.)

- How do you recharge? (Examples: taking a class, having time alone, or asking for help.)

- How do you clutter your mind? (Examples: questioning your decisions, being indecisive, or letting fear block you.)

- What transformation needs to occur? (Examples: changing old habits or patterns, letting go of the past, or taking risks to grow.)

- How can you access needed insights? (Examples: seeking outside help, accessing and trusting your intuition, or reading inspirational books.)

THE POWER TOOL OF BALANCING OUR ARCHETYPES

The archetypes work better when balanced and in tandem. If we have too much of one energy or not enough of another, we can access one or more archetypal energies to bring balance. For example, the King can direct an over-developed Lover who is addicted to pleasure to harness Warrior energy and act with courageous intent to set limits. If our sadistic Warrior becomes abusive, we can access our healthy Lover's compassion and practice empathy. When our overdeveloped Magician is secretive or manipulative, we can call upon the King to foster integrity and authenticity. And if our weakling King needs insight and understanding, we can seek the wise counsel of the insightful Magician. Understanding and harnessing our archetypal energy is another true Power Tool!

HOW DO WE ACTIVATE OUR BALANCED AND POWERFUL SOVEREIGN/KING ENERGY?

Since the Sovereign/King is the steward and leader of the other archetypes, how do we fully activate that balanced and powerful energy? Here are some steps we teach in our workshops and webinars and employ in our men's groups:

1. Fully own your Kingship. Work on embracing the leader/King inside you.

2. Work on integrating your Abdicator and Tyrant King. Change the stories that tell you that you are not powerful, worthy, or effective!

3. Do your own Father Work by learning to father yourself lovingly.

4. Use affirmations and feedback circles to affirm the mature King within you!

5. Practice blessing yourself and others in authentic ways.

6. Practice receiving blessings from others—without deflecting!

RICK

After leaving teaching in 2007, I started my business of teaching, coaching, writing, and public speaking. Just like my father, I believed I could do this all alone. As I worked out of my home, my tyrant King wasn't going to ask anyone for help, and my ignorant, under-developed Magician didn't know what he didn't know. From that unhealthy place, I tried to create a website, logo, videos, Facebook pages, business plan, all while learning how to improve public speaking skills and develop a business. Doing this by myself just didn't work. Floundering and exhausted, I told my men's group that my business was failing—badly.

My group reminded me that I didn't have to do this alone and that I wasn't weak or un-masculine if I asked for help from professionals to assist me. The men helped me access my balanced King who could ask for help to improve the kingdom. That included accessing my healthy Warrior to support my King and fight for what I needed. Drawing upon my insightful Magician, I identified areas of weakness and then hired professionals—webmaster, graphics designer, and virtual assistant. I joined the National Speakers Association, attended seminars, and expanded my network. My healthy Lover infused my work with love. The result of integrating the archetypes resulted in a flourishing, healthier business.

During those times when we don't know what we need and want, especially if we don't have a mission, we can clarify and understand our needs and desires by drawing upon the archetypes. They are essential for men to be fully engaged and committed as fathers. A father needs the Warrior for discipline and limit setting, the Lover to convey compassion and empathy, the Magician to share knowledge and insights, and the King to be a steward in the family.

ACCESSING THE POWER TOOL OF FATHERING

As the primary bearer of King energy in the family, a father works cooperatively with a partner to bless, support, protect, and encourage his children. Without the presence of a healthy King, a father can turn into a tyrant, weakling, or become neglectful. Children's relationships with their father are critical to their emotional well-being and development, just as it is for them to receive wholesome mothering. Since boys need a healthy male role model, the impact of fatherlessness on their lives is horrific. Consider these statistics: 72 percent of adolescent murderers, 70 percent of men in prison, 63 percent of youth suicides, 85 percent of children with behavior disorders, and 71 percent of high school dropouts grew up in homes without a father.[56] Not surprisingly, most of the deadliest mass shootings in America involved males who came from homes with disengaged or absent fathers.

On the flip side, considerable research shows that loving, engaged fathers have a lifelong positive impact on their children's

---

56 Statistics taken from the following: U.S. Department of Health; U.S. Department of Health and Human Services; U.S. Bureau of the Census; Center for Disease Control; Criminal Justice & Behavior; and National Principals Association Report.

development. Children with actively involved father figures are more likely to have higher degrees of success in their careers, better relationships, and an improved ability to handle problems. Their self-esteem is higher, and their levels of anxiety, depression, and behavior problems are lower than children who are raised in homes without dads.

Many of us experienced fathers who were absent, divorced, weak, alcoholic, or workaholic. We did not learn a strong, healthy model of fathering, nor did we learn how to be present for our kids. We can easily pass this father wound onto the next generation—perpetuating this vicious cycle. The only way to break this cycle is to father ourselves in loving, kind, and generative ways. This can happen in a circle of men who see our gifts and hold us accountable to our agreements as fathers. We believe this is critical work for our families and for the world.

LEONARD

When I was six, my father was hospitalized in a mental institution. He remained there for one and a half years. When he was discharged, he returned to the family but left again when I was nine. I felt more fear in his presence, unsure how he would behave. I longed to have a relationship with a father figure, someone who would protect, care for, and love me. Because of my childhood experience, I grew up not fully trusting men.

While living in Australia, I left a job as director of a family therapy center to become a stay-at-home dad for a year when my children were young. At the time my wife was director of a multicultural pre-school. We both had high pressure jobs, and our children needed more care. Since I was a fatherless son of a fatherless son, I was motivated to provide a vastly different experience for my own children.

During that life-changing experience where I was the primary caregiver, I personally witnessed the sharp contrast between growing up without a father/King versus the positive benefits of my being actively involved with my children who are now adults. On one hand, because I felt abandoned, unloved, anxious, and not good enough, I was reluctant to ask for help. On the other hand, my children were more relaxed with themselves and comfortable about coming to me or their mother whenever they needed help. The only drawback to my involvement is that my children weren't as interested in self-development programs. As my son told me, "Living with you, Dad, every day was a day of personal development!"

Since we know the incredible benefits of fathering—and we know the consequences on children who don't have fathers—it is truly absurd that our culture does not value fathering enough. Without role models of emotionally engaged fathers, boys will look to cultural images of masculinity. Those images show up in movies and heroic figures who use violence to solve problems. In the 2015 movie *Avengers: The Age of Ultron*, Hawkeye, the only superhero who was a father, left his pregnant wife and two children at home so he could "save the world." This model produces children who yearn to know their dad. Robert Bly, one of the founders of the men's movement that started in the 70s, stated that a vast number of men suffer from the father wound.

> *It is easier to build strong children than to repair broken men.*
>
> — *Frederick Douglass*

In 1975 a father spent three hours per week engaged with his children (as opposed to nine hours for mothers) as stated in *Time* magazine's May 21, 2018 edition. In 2015 that number for men stretched to seven hours (versus fifteen hours for mothers). When the Kingly fathering is missing from the castle, the results are cat-astrophic. This can be seen even in the animal kingdom.

In 1999 at the Pilanesberg Game Reserve, a wildlife park, Northwest of Johannesburg, South Africa, they had a crisis. Thirty-nine rhinoceroses, 10 percent of the rhino population, were killed. The murderers weren't poachers but elephants, an unusual phenom-enon because elephants were relatively peaceful. The park rangers discovered that young male elephants were behind the killings. The problem started twenty years earlier in a conservation program in Kruger National Park. Because Kruger had too many elephants, the rangers began to cull the herd by killing some of the male bulls and transporting the young elephants to Pilanesberg Game Reserve. As the elephants grew into the teen years, there were no male bulls in the herd. That created a climate for juvenile delinquents to not only terrorize tourists but also to kill rhinos. They had become a gang of pachyderms without role models.

The park rangers decided to bring in a few bull elephants from Kruger National Park. When they arrived, amazing changes occurred. The presence of bigger, older elephants established a new hierarchy as they sparred with the younger elephants. That discouraged them from becoming sexually active, which meant a decrease in testosterone. Less testosterone meant less acting out. Since the bull elephants were introduced, not one rhino has been killed.

That story highlights the importance of older males—even with elephants—in mentoring younger members and steering them away from destructive behaviors. When we access Sovereign energy, we become more relational, emotionally engaged, and committed to our children who yearn to feel protected and hear the precious words, "I love you."

Michael Gurian, author of *The Wonder of Boys*, offers some key principles for fathers:

- Make a conscious decision to be a father. That includes fathering during your partner's pregnancy and the early infancy of your children.

- Practice self-awareness to change and grow as a parent as your children develop and mature. This step includes changing the stories that run in our head about fathering that we learned from our own childhood.

- Become comfortable with your body, gender, sexuality, and senses so you can talk to your children about these important aspects of life when the time comes.

- Develop a desire to communicate with and listen to your children and learn the skills of establishing and maintaining a relationship.

- Create a vision of fathering that includes the ability to not only mentor your children but also let them go to discover their own talents and gifts.[57]

We must reinforce the importance of fathering with other men and help other boys develop mature masculinity. Even if we're not biological fathers, we can bring our Sovereign energy to any number of organizations, like Big Brothers, Boy Scouts, Boys and Girls Clubs, and 4-H Clubs, to name a few. Leonard participated as an assistant Scoutmaster in the Boy Scouts, and Rick volunteered as a mentor for two boys for over ten years in the Big Brothers organization.

The next generation will benefit from the transformative energies of stewardship, power, love, and wisdom. As Moore and

---

57   Gurian, Michael, *The Wonder of Boys*, Tarcher/Putnam, New York, 1997, pp. 113-114.

Gillette write, "We will have a sense of being a centered participant in creating a just, calm, and creative world. We will have a transpersonal devotion not only to our families, our friends, our companies, our causes, our religions, but also to the world." Now that's work for a powerful King!

In the TV series *Game of Thrones* there are seven kingdoms. Each has its own particular qualities with unique kings, warriors, magicians, and lovers. Each of us has created our own special kingdom. We can sit on a throne, isolated from other kingdoms, or we can join forces with other Sovereigns as stewards and create a realm that faces challenges, heals wounds, solves problems, and spreads authentic love and connection.

THE SOVEREIGN/KING STRETCH

1. Describe how you feel and act when you access your Sovereign/King.

2. Describe how you feel and act when your tyrant or weakling King is in charge.

3. What archetypes do you need to develop more fully to become a powerful King?

4. What guidance does your King give now?

5. How does your fathering show up in the world?

6. How can you use the archetypes to strengthen your fathering? (If you are not a father, how can the archetypes help you assist the next generation?)

Chapter Eleven

Applying the Classics Model When Facing Challenges

Unless we learn to know ourselves, we run the danger of destroying ourselves.

— Ja A. Jahannes

I n his first therapy session, Fred faced Leonard and slumped on the couch. His eyes darted to the floor as he talked. "I've suffered from depression for years. My wife finally convinced me to see you. I don't like the idea of coming here, but I promised her that I'd come for one session. I'm the only one who can solve my problem, but I'll listen to what you have to say."

We have heard countless stories from men like Fred. Men have endured anxiety, addictions, violence, and depression for years without seeking help. Some have faced serious health challenges, relationship problems, suicidal thoughts, or spiritual crises without the support of others or any connection to a Higher Power. They suffered in silence. They may have masked their pain through overwork, sex, alcohol, or drugs.

Men may go through a third divorce, have suicidal thoughts, face a quadruple bypass, or drown in alcohol, but their immediate reaction often has been to deny that they have a problem or even blame someone else for causing the pain. They may have spent years avoiding the problem, toughing it out, or trying to fix the problem on their own. However, when the pain of living became more unbearable than the pain of change, they finally sought help.

This chapter speaks to those who need assistance. Rather than suffer alone, we men must break out of a rigid model and toxic behaviors and create a blueprint for healthy masculinity. Asking for help need not be an act of humiliation and defeat but an act of courage, for it takes courage to reach out to a doctor, therapist, minister, friend, or support group. Acknowledging powerlessness over a problem becomes the gateway to healing.

The eight dimensions of the CLASSICS blueprint provide a number of entry points where you can heal wounds, overcome challenges, and evolve. Let's review them.

- Connect with your emotions. You can't heal anything until you first become aware of any pain and discomfort and connect with your feelings. This is the genesis of men's work. Feel it so you can heal it.

- Love yourself enough to risk healing. That includes surmounting the barriers you set up that prevent you from fully loving yourself, your story, your challenges, and others. Open your heart by allowing yourself to be seen, known, and loved.

- Authentically share your pain with others. Real men remove their armor, reveal their shadows, and allow themselves to be vulnerable. These lead to integrity. Be authentic and accountable for your actions and the impacts on others. This builds trust in yourself and with others.

- **S**piritually heal by practicing forgiveness of yourself and others. This leads to a connection with your inner spirit so you can be spirit-driven in all that you do. Develop a spiritual practice that nourishes and sustains you.

- **S**exually awaken your masculinity and connect with your aliveness. As you harness your sexual energy, you will find your passion. Channel your sexuality into a driving force for healing.

- **I**ntentionally create your mission. Turn your wounds into gold that you can share with the world. Being mission driven allows you to access the life you were meant to live. Live each day with your mission in mind.

- **C**ommune with a safe circle or men's group. You do not have to heal alone. To develop and grow as a man, you must do it in the presence of other men. Brotherhood is salvation. Seek the support from other men who also need community.

- **S**overeignly lead with your inner King to access your Warrior, Lover, and Magician as needed. With your mature King in charge, you can overcome problems, heal wounds, and spread love in the world. Stand tall in your King energy and create a sacred kingdom.

Let's return to Fred and the ways that he used the eight dimensions to handle his depression. Attending therapy with Leonard, he shared that his two closest friends had committed suicide.

Not surprisingly, his attitude was to soldier on, as he announced, "Talking doesn't do any good," something he'd heard from his father. Fred's first task was to make a commitment to healing that included learning about feelings and altering his coping mechanism of shutting down. Leonard identified his battle as between the death force (dark shadows) and the light force (inner gold). The deaths Fred faced forced him to suppress feelings and create isolation, whereas the light force emboldened self-expression and connection. To win the battle, Fred had to call upon his inner King and Warrior to take a stand against the tyranny of the death force/depression.

Fred faced the inner challenge and slowly opened up. He revealed heartache not only for his dead friends but for the pain he'd experienced growing up. He needed considerable support to share his grief which overwhelmed him. However, as he moved through his emotions, he accessed his Lover to accept and forgive himself for his past, realizing he had adopted the model of masculinity handed down by his father. The grieving process helped Fred feel his heart pump with life.

As he worked on himself, he reached out to connect with Joyce, his wife of thirty years. She yearned for more intimacy. They hadn't had sex in two years and didn't even talk about the lack of intimacy. That changed when Fred began showing his authentic, vulnerable self. His compassion and love awakened a desire to touch and be touched. That desire flowed into their sex lives which experienced a rebirth. Joyce's comments to Fred summed up her delight at his evolution. "I've never felt this close to you in all the years we've been married."

While Fred made use of the support and encouragement of a therapist to heal and embrace a new roadmap of masculinity, some men need a larger community to facilitate healing.

ADDICTIONS AND COMPULSIONS

Substance abuse not only affects the physical health of men but also severely impacts family relationships and employment. The National Council on Alcoholism and Drug Dependence states that alcoholism is the third leading lifestyle-related cause of death in America and that opiate addiction, with drugs such as heroin, morphine, opium, or Oxycodone, is rising at an alarming rate.

We have worked with countless men in recovery, including those with sexual compulsions. Rick was also involved with Al-Anon for years. Twelve-Step programs, which include many of the dimensions of the CLASSICS Model, help men overcome a variety of addictions and compulsions. These groups offer a forum for men to face their denial, receive support, and work with a sponsor. The Twelve Steps include a strong spiritual element that asks men to recognize that they have no control over their addictions (Step One), that they believe in a Higher Power who can help and to whom they can surrender control (Steps Two and Three), and that they seek enlightenment and connection with a Higher Power through prayer and meditation (Step Eleven). Men are asked to be vulnerable and authentic while taking a personal inventory so that they can self-correct (Steps Four and Ten) and become accountable for past deeds by making amends (Step Eight). Finally, men are asked to step into the community and carry this message to others who face similar problems (Step Twelve).[58] In essence, men are asked to adopt a new code of behavior and live a life of mission.

HARRY

A tall, thirty-five-year-old plumber with a mustache, Harry felt compelled to attend group therapy. Actually, his wife Helen

---

58 Anonymous, *Twelve Steps and Twelve Traditions,* Alcoholics Anonymous World Services, Inc. New York, 1952, pp. 5-9.

demanded that he seek help and change or else face a divorce. She had recently discovered that he'd spent $3000 over several months on phone sex. At first, Harry denied his problem, saying that someone had stolen his credit card information. His wife, fed-up with his lies, gave him an ultimatum: Come clean and seek help or get out. With two young children, Harry did not want to lose his family. Reluctantly, he attended a men's therapy group led by Leonard.

Facing his problem, Harry felt deeply ashamed for squandering money that his family desperately needed, for letting down his wife and family whom he loved, and for getting hooked on phone sex with other women. Once he opened up to the group, he felt tremendous relief that he could unburden himself about feeling "fucked up."

Over time, he started taking charge of his life. He talked about his difficulty being sexually intimate with his wife. For him, it was more thrilling to get off with anonymous women on the phone. He began to identify compulsive behaviors, such as secretly watching hours of porn that impacted his relationship. His sexual addiction had slowly eroded his interest in his wife, leaving her feeling rejected.

During the course of the group, he made the intention to connect with Helen and tell the truth, not all that easy for a man who lied to stay out of trouble. The other men in the group called him on any bullshit and kept him accountable to his word. At the same time, the men supported him through his struggles to create a loving, intimate marriage and reinforced his stretches, such as attending couple's counseling with Helen and a Twelve-Step recovery program. Committed to the heavy lifting, Harry slowly re-discovered passion with his wife.

The changes did not occur overnight. However, Harry leaned into the dimensions that were missing in his life. He moved away from objectifying women, which had caused him to diminish intimacy with his wife. He began to identify with his inner King and moved toward connection, love, authenticity, mature sexuality, intentionality, and community. Not surprisingly, Harry's healing journey spurred the other men in the group to change and heal.

MALE VIOLENCE

 LEONARD

Many years ago, I visited my mother who lived on the southside of Chicago. When I left her house, I walked toward my parked car. I stopped in my tracks when I heard a woman scream. Several houses down, a man had pinned a woman on a car and was hitting her. My immediate impulse was to shout, "Hey!" hoping the man would stop and the woman would escape.

The man immediately turned his attention away from the woman and began walking toward me. In his hands he jiggled a large bundle of keys and showed them to me in a menacing way. "Do you have a problem?" he sneered.

I remained frozen. Clearly, I did have a problem. This dude was preparing to punch my face with a fist full of keys.

As he came nearer, he continued jiggling the keys in his hand and repeated the question, "Do you have a problem?"

I glanced at the woman whom he had been striking. She remained frozen, watching us.

When he was about 10 feet away, he asked again, while jiggling his keys, "Do you have a problem?"

"Yes," I said. "I have a problem."

"What's your problem," he barked.

"I'm the problem," I said. I don't know why I said that at the time, maybe it was my training as a therapist to defuse conflict, but it was the only thing that came to me.

He stopped in his track. He became confused trying to sort out what I had just said.

To get the point across, I said again, "I'm the problem."

He looked at me like I was the crazy one and said, "Yeah, you're the problem. You better take care of it."

He shook his head and left me alone. He rejoined the woman and together they walked up the street toward an apartment complex, not saying anything further. As they disappeared into the night, I assumed they were living together, and that this wasn't their first rodeo.

I've thought about that incident many times. I wondered if he had a gun, would I still be alive. Fortunately, my use of words averted violence and stopped the man from beating the woman or me. But it made me ponder the larger question: why are men violent and what can we do about it?

With the rise in domestic violence and mass shootings, men's violence deserves special consideration. While this male violence deserves its own book, we'll briefly review the complex interaction of biology, psychology, and social conditioning.

Biologically, the differences between male and female brains and hormones clearly impact behavior. Female brains are organized more efficiently for speech and reading whereas male brains are better organized for visual/spatial functioning. On the whole, women tend to use verbal aggression while men become more physical. As well, males have 10-20 times more testosterone than females, and that hormone decreases the role of serotonin, the neurotransmitter which inhibits aggressive behavior.

During puberty, testosterone production in boys increases 30-fold. Since this increase is often linked to changes in mood and behavior such as aggression and risk taking, adolescent males are more prone to acting out violently when they don't utilize other outlets.

As boys develop psychologically, they begin to discriminate between masculine and feminine behaviors, avoiding qualities typically associated with femininity such as vulnerability, nurturance, sensitivity, gentleness, sweetness, humility, affection, tenderness, and emotional intimacy. As a result, men selectively incorporate behaviors that are considered more manly such as being tough, unemotional, aggressive, even violent.

Since anger was a feeling that men allowed themselves to experience or express, other emotions like sadness and fear were suppressed. Emotions that showed vulnerability were either stuffed emotions or projected outward. Suppressing emotions often came out as passive-aggressive behavior while projection led to blaming others or explosive outbursts.

When anger is not handled appropriately, it triggers an unhealthy chain of events. It can lead to loneliness, isolation, and depression. Or when anger is externalized into blaming others, it can translate into rage. As the old saying goes, irritation unresolved leads to anger, anger unresolved leads to rage, rage unresolved leads to violence and prison—one of the reasons why 93 percent of prisoners in the United States are male.

If anger hijacks our thoughts and dominates our life, we must learn to master the emotion versus letting the anger master us. Healthy anger can be an energizing force that tells us something is wrong in a situation, or our boundaries have been crossed. We can then exert control of an out-of-control situation and, instead of overreacting, we can choose how to respond.

In addition to a man's biology and psychology, we have to recognize the impact of social conditioning. American culture celebrates aggression as a characteristic of manhood. Sports, politics, and business are dominated by men who represent competition, aggression, and winning at all costs. Aggression is rewarded; passivity is demeaned.

"Real" men in movies are represented by those who use violence to solve problems. James Bond, Jack Reacher, and Jason Bourne are examples of tough, angry men using brawn not relationship skills to handle conflict. Young boys watching these movies, absorb the message that violence is a form of establishing and proving manhood.

Using the CLASSICS Model, we can connect with our body, senses, and emotions whenever we feel angry. We can monitor and regulate anger and channel it into a motivating force for change. Consider the story of Edgar.

EDGAR

As part of his treatment for domestic violence, Edgar was mandated to attend anger management classes and counseling. He had beaten his wife and stalked her when she moved out of their apartment. She had taken out a restraining order against him. While he attended court-ordered classes to manage his anger, he worked with Leonard who initially assessed any risk of violence. Leonard stressed the importance of complying with the restraining order and ensuring the safety of Edgar's wife with a "no-threat, no violence" contract. The external constraints of the court provided the impetus for Edgar to address his problems with anger. Therapy reinforced the need to manage his aggression because anger had become the master of his life, so much so that he hurt his wife whom he loved. Thus began Edgar's intense program of self-mastery.

He began to identify his pattern of victimizing others, especially when he felt out of control and vulnerable. He learned to recognize his triggers and his response and began employing techniques to cool down, tap into compassion, and communicate more effectively. That necessitated Edgar's accessing his inner King to ask for help, connect with his emotions, relate vulnerably and authentically, and being accountable for his behavior. He adopted a mission to heal himself and create a safe place for others. Not easy work for a man who had depended on his fists to survive as a boy in a gang-ridden neighborhood.

While Edgar and his wife eventually divorced, his commitment to self-mastery led him to personal development seminars and men's groups where he inspired other men to overcome problems with anger. As Edgar put it, "I was a mean son-of-a-bitch, but after lots of hard work, I'm a kinder, more loving man."

HEALING TRAUMA

Like, Fred, Harry, and Edgar, most of us have experienced trauma, which is defined by the American Psychological Association as, "an emotional response to a terrible event like an accident, rape, or natural disaster." Many of us suffer silently from the effects of childhood trauma—violence, fatherlessness, alcoholism, drug abuse, sexual or physical abuse, and poverty. These types of early life experiences are known as Adverse Childhood Experiences (ACEs). The original assessment tool for ACEs is a ten-item questionnaire, the result of a study conducted by the Centers for Disease Control and Prevention (CDC) and Kaiser Permanente from 1995-1997 with over 17,000 adult participants. The assessment tool (Felitti et al., 1998) is a 10-item questionnaire used to measure childhood trauma. The simple test helps you evaluate childhood adverse experiences by giving you an ACE Score.[59]

According to ACE researchers, an ACE score of 4 or more presents serious problems. The likelihood of chronic pulmonary lung disease increases 390 percent; hepatitis 240 percent; depression 460 percent; suicide 1,220 percent. Serious indeed! These are but a few of the deleterious effects that can result from higher ACE Scores.

Rick's ACE Score was 5 (out of ten possible), Leonard's was 6. Clearly, both of us learned the survival skills necessary to power through such impediments to find success and validation. In a real sense, it saved our lives. But, as a result, we both still struggle today with the sense that we are valued for what we do, rather than who we are. We believe this is common among men. Each of us

59 https://americanspcc.org/take-the-aces-quiz/

processes our trauma differently and employ a variety of survival skills when we were young that helped us adapt to situations that might not be survivable. However, some of those lifesaving patterns block us from being present, vulnerable, and aware.

The latest theory about trauma is encapsulated in Polyvagal Theory which states that traumas become trapped in our bodies and brains. Therefore, an awareness of our bodies show us the way out of patterns that no longer serve us such as codependence, people pleasing, over-aggression, substance abuse, and so on. Learning to listen to our bodies pays powerful dividends. When dealing with such traumas, the CLASSICS Model encourages connection to emotions, acceptance and love of ourselves, speaking our truth authentically, and setting intentions that are life affirming This is best done in community with other men who can support us to become the King of our lives.

RICK

In doing my own recovery work, I recently created a "Trauma Journal." Digging into my past, I recorded 76 traumatic experiences in my life that I could recall! They varied from two near-death experiences survived while young, to the loss of my son through miscarriage, To the loss of my father at age 38, to being made fun of and abandoned by friends due to my religious beliefs, to my two painful divorces. I experienced deaths of strangers by coming upon accidents several times and was asked to help move bodies in two incidents. Even in utero, I experienced tragedy as my mother came upon her beloved sister's body after she shot herself in the head in my mother's kitchen while my mom was three months pregnant with me. All of these incidents had an impact on me—my feelings of safety were particularly challenged by these traumatic experiences.

To help with my healing, I went to a Somatic Experiencing (SE) Therapist for a year. She helped me connect my traumatic survival mechanisms to my body in unique and powerful ways. My therapist noticed small movements that occurred in my body as I talked about my traumatic experiences. She pointed out that I had showed amazing resiliency by getting through these traumas, but that those very same mechanisms were now holding me back from experiencing greater freedom and deeper intimacy with my loved ones. I found great comfort in that SE exploration and healed deep trauma in this way.

I used all the CLASSICS Model behaviors to help me heal. Connecting with my therapist, I experienced intense emotions associated with these events. As I shared my trauma authentically with my partner and friends, I saw how my sexuality was impacted, and learned to love myself fully. I continued to attend my men's circle and shared freely what I was discovering about myself. Accessing my inner King, I activated my Mission and intention to free myself from these buried events and found my rightful throne in the midst of the carnage in my life. Truly lifesaving work. I am grateful to Leonard and so many others who helped me through this difficult time. Even so, that work is ongoing for me.

SEXUAL ABUSE

One of the deepest traumas men deal with is sexual abuse. That wound often stems from the father wound, the deep yearning to really know a father and to be loved unconditionally, blessed, and respected. When a man is not seen and heard by his father, he becomes vulnerable to exploitation by men (or women) offering attention. This can lead to abusive behaviors, including sexual abuse.

Both of us have friends who were sexually molested by Catholic priests (known as fathers!). These friends were altar boys at the time, and both did not have close relationships with their dads. Back then, few questioned the authority of a priest, especially innocent young boys. Males especially carry deep shame about being violated by an older man and often carry those emotions to the grave, rarely revealing their stories. Even so, we've heard dozens of horror stories from men who've courageously shared painful memories. Rick's father was an example, as he carried his abuse story for almost 50 years before revealing his pain to Rick just before his death.

These men not only suffered the usual psychological trauma associated with abuse, they also experienced the murder of their sacred selves. Recovery often takes a lifetime because they have to reconcile how a loving God could allow his representatives to molest them. This issue has not only rocked the Catholic Church, it has shown up in many arenas in society. Consider these statistics:

- Bureau of Justice Statistics (BJS) findings suggest that in one year alone more than 70,000 prisoners were sexually abused or raped.[60]

- 16 percent of men experience sexual abuse by the age of 18. These reports are widely thought to be underestimated because males fear they will be thought of as unmanly or gay if they report these incidents.[61]

- An estimated 60,000 males are sexually assaulted annually outside of prison.[62]

MATT

A healing circle on a leadership training weekend was led by Rick that took place in a former seminary. A participant, Matt, shared the painful story about his sexual abuse as a teenager that had occurred in that very chapel thirty-six years before. Matt's voice

---

60 Sexual Victimization in State and Federal Prisons Reported by Inmates, 2007

61 U.S. Centers for Disease Control, 2005

62 U.S. Department of Justice, 2017

shook with a mixture of rage and sadness as he disclosed that he'd been in the seminary training to become a Catholic priest when his mentor, one of his teachers and a leader of the seminary, began to touch him inappropriately. He felt powerless to stop this, which culminated with the priest bending Matt over the altar to have sex with him. This had occurred more than once.

Matt's pain was palpable as he struggled to describe the violation. "He took my innocence and made me question my sexual orientation for years. The worst part was that he damaged my spirituality and my relationship with God and the church. That's the hardest part of my recovery. I'm fifty-five and still can't forgive him or God. After leaving the seminary, I've struggled to find a safe place in this world."

Matt had years of therapy after leaving the seminary but didn't quite feel complete in his healing. The circle suggested that Matt pick a man to play his abuser and another man to play a loving God. The man who portrayed the abusing priest was placed between Matt and God. In order to reclaim his healthy sexuality and his relationship with his spirituality, Matt had to get past the priest who had raped him and stolen his power.

The circle supported Matt as he connected with his rage and grief. He first focused his anger on the abuser. "Get out of my life! Fuck you for fucking me over. Fuck you for taking away my love of God and my church. Fuck you for making sex dirty! I take back my power."

The circle of men encouraged Matt to tap into his rage and tell his abuser what he felt until he knew in his guts that this man would never again stand between him and his God or his sexual beauty. Matt shouted and screamed at the one portraying the abuser until that man fell to the floor, leaving Matt standing in front of the one playing God who held out loving arms. Matt sobbed tears of relief that he had finally confronted his abuser. The man standing in for God then spoke, "Matt, you are a sacred, sexual being. You are beautiful. I love you." God repeated these affirmations several times while embracing Matt.

Matt melted into these powerful words. After some time, he faced the circle of men and thanked them. "I feel God's love and acceptance once again. I've waited a long time to reclaim my sexuality and power." He was asked to share a declaration that he could now hold. With bright eyes, Matt announced, "I am a sacred, loving man, and my God loves me!"

With the support of the circle, Matt employed several CLASSICS tools to help his healing—connecting with the circle of men, recovering his spiritual connection with God, sharing authentically, healing sexually, and accessing his inner King.

A final note: Matt returned to the Catholic faith soon after the weekend and dedicated himself to helping survivors of priest sexual abuse.

HEALING THE FATHER WOUND

Every boy is born with a hole in his belly. If his dad didn't fill it, it festers and becomes an aching black hole—one that he'll spend his waking hours trying to fill. Mostly with things that do him more harm than good.

— *Charles Martin*

Father wounds run deep and create incredible suffering for men. If we didn't have a father figure who was actively involved or emotionally engaged in our lives, we must access the energy of other healthy males to find our own inner father, much like Matt. That means learning to parent ourselves, give ourselves the messages we desperately wanted to hear, and receive loving words from other men. Most of us need to hear these messages: "I am loved unconditionally. I am respected. I am valuable, talented, and lovable."

MANUEL

After every ManKind Project training weekend, a follow-up Homecoming Celebration occurs where the men are publicly welcomed home by the staff of the weekend and the families and friends of the men who participated. For this weekend, twenty-six men, who had completed the training, attended with their loved ones and the staff. As the leader of the weekend, Rick asked the men to share their stories.

The first one to speak was Manuel, a short Latino man with bulging muscles and bright blue eyes. He looked directly at the 120 people present and took a deep breath. He then spoke. "Before I came to my weekend, I hit rock bottom. I never knew my dad and had spent my life looking for him on street corners, in a bottle, and at the tip of a needle. I now live in a halfway house where I receive treatment for drug and alcohol addiction. I wondered if my life was worth living. I felt flawed and unredeemable."

Manuel wiped his eyes. "This weekend changed my life. I found out that I was lovable, and that I can create a good life for myself, complete with a loving father and mother who live inside me! I could own my story and feel my feelings and not lose myself in shame. I also found amazing connections with the men at the training. I never felt so loved and accepted. My heart opened wide."

Manuel's tears flowed down his cheeks. "I feel like I've grown into a new man. I am committed to my sobriety and healing. Now I have many men to help me do this. A miracle!"

Just as the audience thought Manuel had finished his sharing, he wiped his eyes, then smiled. "When I got back to my halfway house Sunday night, the front desk called me, saying I had a visitor. I walked to the reception area, confused. I rarely had visitors. I spotted an old man sitting in the waiting area. When I approached him, he looked up. As soon as I saw his eyes—*my* eyes—I knew he was my father! We hugged, father and son. On the very same weekend that I was reborn by claiming my inner loving father in

213

front of the men on that training, my biological father showed up for the first time in my life. Another miracle!"

When Manuel finished speaking, those who attended shared tears of joy with him. His smile and words electrified the audience who broke out in prolonged applause.

When the applause died down, Manuel added, "I don't know if my father will continue to be there for me or not. But I do know that it no longer really matters. *From now on, I live my life fully for me!*"

Manuel willingly embraced the dimensions. He emotionally connected with an open heart, authentically shared with others, and intentionally created a vision of re-parenting himself in a community of men. No doubt, there will be ongoing challenges. However, he now had a blueprint to continue his evolution up the mountain as a new man. His journey, like that of other awakening men, inspires us to continually evolve in the world. Manuel's use of CLASSICS Power tools was lifesaving for him and even transformative for those in attendance that day.

Another way to heal our father wound is to learn how to be healthy elders. We are not taught how to age gracefully. And we often know little about how to use our hard-earned wisdom and experience to elder younger men. And as we elder younger men, we elder ourselves, helping to heal that father wound.

HEALTHY AGING AND ELDERHOOD

A human being would certainly not grow to be 70 or 80 years old if this longevity had no meaning for the species to which he belongs. The afternoon of human life must also have a significance of its own and cannot be merely a pitiful appendage to life's morning.

— Carl Jung

214

If you are pining for youth, I think it produces a stereotypical old man because you only live in memory, you live in a place that doesn't exist. I think aging is an extraordinary process whereby you become the person that you always should have been.

— *David Bowie*

Both Jung and Bowie above share insights into how we can bypass the stereotypical old man syndrome or see our mature years as a pitiful appendage to our lives. Instead, we are invited to step fully into our eldership in significant ways, especially to serve younger men who are hungry for father figures. That's how you become the man you "always should have been." This allows us to flower into healthy, generative, powerful Eldership. The world—especially men—desperately needs such Elders. The liberation that follows is described beautifully in the quote below:

🜨 RICK

One way I expressed my healthy elder was to run a Father/Daughter Weekend for 25 years with my own daughters. During that summer weekend, I witnessed men and their daughters bonding and healing in beautiful ways. Connection and love abounded, as did community and mission. On each weekend, the fathers would connect around a campfire while their daughters were doing empowering activities with older daughters. During that Father's Circle, men expressed their pain, bewilderment, and fear of fathering their daughters well. For example, some men stopped hugging their daughters when they reached puberty out of fear that they would be perceived as abusers. Some men carried the message, often from their wives, that they did not know how to parent a daughter well. Others dealt with the pain and loss of divorce which lessened the time spent with their daughters.

In all cases, these beautiful men eldered each other, listening attentively with each taking turns sharing and emoting. They created a loving, healing community of connection as they shared from their hearts and souls. Realizing they were not alone in their quest to father well, they welcomed each other as powerful Kings. Witnessing and experiencing those Father's Circles each year brought me tremendous joy as I eldered younger dads through the years.

We invite you to mine your authentic Eldership, find other wise elders to spend time with, and learn from and emulate them. Find younger men hungry for wise Eldership and mentor them.

When men who are isolated, overwhelmed, depressed, anxious, or even suicidal connect with a supportive man or group of men, transformation occurs. Sometimes they need to start with one-on-one counseling or mentoring to shift old patterns. Power tools come in many forms and from many sources! Elders serve the community as well as themselves.

🝊 RICK

I was an active member of the Big Brothers organization for ten years. During that time, I mentored two young fatherless boys. I recently realized that I was actually accessing my elder to do this. My first Little Brother was named Kent. I worked with him for six years. Five years into our connection, he was diagnosed with a grapefruit sized cancerous tumor at the base of his spine. It appeared to be inoperable until a gifted surgeon stepped in to perform a miracle. Kent's tumor was removed, and he retained the use of his legs.

During his recovery, I visited him in the hospital most every day. I'd have to lay on my back on the floor to see him as he was in a special bed facing down so his surgical wound could heal from the inside out. During his convalescence, I promised Kent that if he recovered fully enough, I would take him out west for a few weeks in the summer to camp and take a raft trip down the mighty Colorado River.

When Kent had an amazing recovery, we took that trip. He had never been out of Wisconsin before, so the Rocky Mountains, the Grand Canyon, and red rock country of Utah were a revelation to him. We hiked and swam and rafted for three weeks in glorious celebration of his recovery.

Shortly after our return, Kent entered the same high school that I taught in. He would stop into my classroom just to say hi and to report on how his transition to high school was going. A month into the school year, Kent had a tragic dirt bike accident, and he was killed instantly. I was devastated, as was his mother. I struggled to understand how Kent survived a close call with cancer only to die a few short months later in a senseless accident.

I turned to my men's group for eldering. They held me and loved me through this trauma and helped me worked through my anger with God for allowing such a loss. They helped me express my grief and anger authentically and they also reminded me of my spiritual practices that had seen me through other traumatic experiences.

Kent's mother asked me to perform his funeral service since I was a minister at the time. I spoke of my love for Kent and his family at the funeral to over 500 folks—mostly students. I didn't realize until then that my eldering had impacted many more people than Kent.

We could fill several books with stories about men who left the isolation of a lonely, cold cave and entered the warmth of shared brotherhood. In that shared space, we recognize the inherent beauty of men. Together we have the power to heal and soar!

We invite you into the welcoming arms of men willing to exit their lonely caves, connect with each other, and practice the healthy behaviors together. These practices will help you evolve and to build a better, emotionally connected, and fulfilling life. As men willingly move from the outmoded model of manhood and embrace the eight CLASSICS dimensions, their lives will change forever.

THE HOME STRETCH

1. What messages have you yearned to hear from your father?

2. Turn these "you" messages into affirmations. (Examples: I am wanted and desired, I am loved, I am blessed, I am good enough, etc.) Say these daily to yourself.

3. Name a current problem you are struggling with. How can you apply the eight dimensions to resolve the problem?

    a. Connect with emotions and relationships.

    b. Love with an open heart.

    c. Authentically relate vulnerably with accountability and Integrity.

    d. Spiritually connect within and with others.

    e. Sexually awaken the masculine self.

    f. Intentionally live a Mission of Service.

    g. Commune with a circle of men.

    h. Sovereignly lead with an inner King.

4. What aspects of your life do you wish to celebrate?

5. How can you celebrate your awakened masculine self?

Epilogue

Knowing is not enough; we must apply. Willing is not enough; we must do..."

— Johann Wolfgang von Goethe

While working on this book, we found many opportunities to talk about masculinity with men and women.

 RICK

When I gave a talk to a group of a hundred men and women, I asked the group, "What does it mean to be a man today?"

A seventy-year-old woman raised her hand and announced, "In my opinion, men are assholes!"

Seeing the pain in her eyes, I replied, "There are a lot of women who have been hurt by men. Our blueprint for healthy masculinity is changing that. When we are actively changing our lives to be loving, compassionate, and emotionally connected to ourselves and others we will spend less time hurting each other, women, and children."

 LEONARD

While flying to Berkeley for a conference recently, I talked with a young man, Robert, who was sitting next to me on the plane. At twenty-three, he was training to become a physical therapist. When I told him about our book on masculinity, his eyes sparkled.

"I have been listening to podcasts on men."

He then shared his ideas about what it means to be a man. "I believe gender is more fluid than we think and that men and women should relate as co-equals. My girlfriend is more emotionally intelligent and relational, and I want to learn those skills so I can lead a balanced life."

Robert represents the hope of a new generation of men less constrained by traditional roles and more willing to embrace the eight dimensions. Success in his eyes meant having relationships that are open, authentic, and loving. Meeting men like him gives us hope for our future and prompts us to ask important questions: What is the future of men? If evolution is a given, where will it take us? What can we do now?

Scott Griffiths and Eric Elfman address these questions in *Beyond Genius: The 12 Essential Traits of Today's Renaissance Men*. They write, "… the Renaissance Man has within him the vital need to push humanity forward, empowering people to take control of their lives and creating more productive relationships…. His insatiable curiosity and vision of the future let him see how life could be improved. His passionate need to create and share his work, as well as his courage to take risks and his perseverance, are nearly always performed in pursuit of a more perfect world. And in seeing possibilities and solutions that most do not, in diverging from and challenging the norm, the Renaissance Man is able to push society and knowledge into the future."[63]

As we create our future, we highlight five key areas that call us. Think of these as sacred quests of modern men.

---

63   Griffiths, Scott and Elfman, Eric, *Beyond Genius: The 12 Essential Traits of Today's Renaissance Men*, AuthorHouse, Bloomington, IN, 2013, pp. 40-41.

1. **Choose the principles and values we want to claim.** We can embrace some of the traditional masculine traits that benefit men and society—strength, courage, empowerment, assertiveness, protection, loyalty, and problem solving. We can also develop other qualities that are not typically viewed as masculine but create balance and wholeness—empathy, vulnerability, emotional intelligence, relational skills, spirituality, and the ability to acknowledge problems and ask for help.

2. **Transform male-female relationships.** We acknowledge, respect, and balance our feminine and masculine energies to create respectful connections as co-equals. That dynamic involves creating a safe, sacred place to courageously share our passion and love men and masculinity AND women and femininity.

3. **Reinforce the importance of fathering and eldering.** As fathers, we become not only actively involved but also emotionally engaged and more relational as we raise and empower our children to lead productive, happy, and fulfilled lives. *No one change will catapult humanity forward more quickly than positive, loving fathering and eldering.* We'll embrace love for our own and everyone else's children, no matter the race, color, creed, or gender.

4. **Promote male friendships and connections.** We make the commitment to challenge the norm of male relationships that are isolated and competitive and to establish a brotherhood of men who support, encourage, and love each other as brothers, fathers, grandfathers, and sons.

5. **Heal our individual and collective traumas.** We dive deeply into our traumas to reclaim our vibrancy, gain resilience, put our wounds into perspective, and relate more effectively in relationships.

With excitement, we dare to imagine a future where we men are committed to expanding the eight dimensions of the CLASSICS Model and employing these dimensions in service to these five sacred quests. When we are connecting to emotions and relationships, loving with an open heart, authentically sharing, practicing spirituality, attuning sexually, intentionally fulfilling a Mission of Service, creating community, and living as a healthy Sovereign/King, we can transform ourselves and the world.

Goethe's opening quotation stated, "Knowing is not enough; we must apply." We invite you to join us on this quest, harness the eight dimensions, and incorporate a blueprint for healthy masculinity.

We end with a haiku from our brother, Carl Foster, who wrote this on a recent men's training.

Good men gathering
Much to discover within
The path begins here.

Men's Resources

MEN'S ORGANIZATIONS

THE BOYS TO MEN MENTORING NETWORK, SAN DIEGO, CA

Website: boystomen.org
A national nonprofit organization dedicated to supporting father-less boys through mentoring.

A CALL TO MEN

Website: acalltomen.org
A Call to Men offers trainings and educational resources to transform society by promoting healthy, respectful manhood.

THE GOOD MEN PROJECT

Website: goodmenproject.com
The Good Men Project is a website that provides a wide range of articles about men's changing roles from a variety of perspectives about masculinity.

ILLUMAN

Website: Illuman.org
Illuman is a nonprofit organization that offers men's programs centered in ritual experiences rather than in conceptual teachings.

MAN ENOUGH

Website: manenough.com
Man Enough offers podcasts and posts to undefine traditional roles and traits of masculinity so that men will realize their potential as humans and their capacity for connection.

MANKIND PROJECT

Website: ManKindProject.org
The ManKind Project, an international nonprofit men's training organization with 37 years of promoting transformative work for men, offers a range of courses, weekend programs, and weekly men's groups.

MEN'S DIVISION INTERNATIONAL

Website: mentordiscoverinspire.org
Men's Division International is a nonprofit organization that offers weekend retreats for men (Legacy Discovery Events) and weekly support groups afterwards.

MENLIVING

Website: menliving.org
MenLiving delivers programs and experiences to help create a world of healthy, intentional connected men who can heal and thrive.

NATIONAL AT-HOME DAD NETWORK

Website: athomedad.org
The National At-Home Network, a national nonprofit organization for at-home dads, empowers fathers and champions a culture that recognizes them as capable and competent parents.

NATIONAL ORGANIZATION FOR MEN AGAINST SEXISM

Website: nomas.org
The National Organization for Men Against Sexism is an activist group of men and women who support positive changes for men.

STERLING INSTITUTE

Website: sterling-institute.com
The Sterling Institute of Relationships is a for-profit organization that offers weekends for heterosexual men only, focusing on traditional, modern concepts of masculinity, femininity, sex, marriage, success, and lifestyle.

VICTORIES FOR MEN

Website: victoriesformen.org
Victories, a nonprofit organization, supports men through weekend and group programs that lead to deeper self-awareness, greater self-confidence, stronger relationships, and greater connection to themselves and community.

WEBINARS

The authors have created a series of 9 webinars that highlight the CLASSICS Model and its uses in helping men evolve. Access these at our website: https://powertoolsformen.org/webinar-page

BOOK RESOURCES BY SUBJECT

FATHERING

- Leving, Jeffrey, *Father's Rights*, Basic Books, New York. 1997.

- Osherson, Samuel, *Finding Our Fathers*, Free Press, New York. 1986.

- Popenoe, David, *Life Without Father*, Free Press, New York. 1996.

- Pruett, Kyle, *The Nurturing Father: Journey Toward the Complete Man*, Warner, New York. 1987.

- Scull, Charles, *Fathers, Sons, and Daughters: Exploring Fatherhood, Renewing the Bond*, Jeremy Tarcher, Los Angeles, 1992.

LEADERSHIP AND HEALING

- *Brown*, Brené, *Daring Greatly: How the Courage to Be Vulnerable Transforms the Way We Live, Love, Parent, and Lead*, Avery, New York, 2015.

- Cashman, Kevin, *Leadership from the Inside Out*, Berrit-Koehler Publishing, Oakland, CA, 2017.

- Goleman, Daniel, *Emotional Intelligence: Why It Can Matter More Than IQ*, Bantam, New York, 2005.

- Quinn, Robert E., *Change the World: How Ordinary People Can Accomplish Extraordinary Results*, Jossey-Bass, San Francisco, CA, 2000.

- Robbins, Mike, *Focus on the Good Stuff: The Power of Appreciation*, John Wiley & Sons, San Francisco, CA, 2007.

- Robbins, Mike, *Be Yourself, Everyone Else is Already Taken: Transform Your Life with the Power of Authenticity*, Jossey-Bass, San Francisco, CA, 2009.

- Robbins, Mike, *Nothing Changes Until You Do: A Guide to Self-Compassion and Getting Out of Your Own Way*, Hay House, Carlsbad, CA, 2015.

- Scott, Susan, *Fierce Leadership: A Bold Alternative to the Worst "Best" Practices of Business Today*, Crown Business, New York, 2009.

MALE CONNECTIONS

- Kauth, Bill, *A Circle of Men: The Original Manual for Men's Support Groups*, St. Martin's Press, New York, 1992.

- Tiger, Lionel, *Men in Groups, Third Edition*, Routledge Publishers, New York, 2017.

MANAGING EMOTIONS

- Pert, Candace, *Molecules of Emotion: Why You Feel the Way You Feel,* Scribner, New York, 1997.

- Real, Terry, *I Don't Want to Talk About It: Overcoming the Secret Legacy of Male Depression,* Scribner, New York, 1997.

MEN'S WORK

- Addis, Michael, *Invisible Man: Men's Inner Lives in the Consequences of Silence*, Times Books, New York, 2011.

- Baldoni, Justin, *Man Enough: Undefining My Masculinity*, Harper One, New York, 2021.

- Betcher, R. William, & Pollack, William, *In a Time of Fallen Heroes*. Guildford Press, New York, 1993.

- Bly, Robert, *Iron John: A Book about Men*, Addison-Wesley, New York, 1990.

- Bly, Robert, Hillman, James, & Meade, Michael, *The Rag and Bone Shop of the Heart: Poems for Men*, Harper Collins, New York, 1992.

- Bradshaw, John, *Healing the Shame That Binds You*, HCI Books, Deerfield Beach, FL, 2005.

- Broniec, Rick, *A Passionate Life: 7 Steps for Reclaiming Your Passion, Purpose and Joy*, Create Space, San Bernardino, CA, 2011.

- Farrell, Warren, *Why Men Are the Way They Are*, Berkeley, New York, 1988.

- Joseph, Frederick, *Patriarchy Blues: Reflections on Manhood*, Harper Perennial, New York, 2022.

- Greene, Mark, *The Little #Metoo Book for Men*, ThinkPlay Partners, New York, 2018.

- Gilligan, James, *Violence: Reflections on a National Epidemic*, Vintage Books, New York, 1999.

- Goldberg, Herb, *What Men Really Want*, Signet, New York, 1991.

- hooks, bell, *The Will to Change: Man, Masculinity, and Love*, Atria books, New York, 2004.

- Kauth, Bill, *A Circle of Men: The Original Manual for Men's Support Groups*, St. Martin's Press, New York, 1992.

- Kaufman, Michael, *The Time Has Come: Why Men Must Join the Gender Equality Revolution*, Counterpoint, Berkeley, 2019.

- Keen, Sam, *Fire in the Belly: On Being a Man*, Bantam, New York, 1991.

- Kipnis, Aaron, *Knights Without Armor*, G. P. Putnam, New York, 1991.

- Krasner, Barbara, *Toxic Masculinity*, Greenhaven Publishing, New York, 2020.

- Kritsberg, Wayne, Lee, John, & Bliss, Shepherd, *A Quiet Strength Meditations on the Masculine Soul,* Bantam Books, New York, 1994.

- Lee, John, *The Flying Boy: Healing the Wounded Man*, Health Communications, Deerfield Beach, FL, 1989.

- Levant, Ronald, & Pollack, William, Ed. *A New Psychology of Men*, Basic Books, New York, 1995.

- Lew, Mike, *Victims No Longer: Men Recovering from Incest and Other Sexual Child Abuse*. Harper & Row, N.Y. 1990.

- Mark, Robert, & Portugal, Buddy, *Victories of the Heart: The Inside Story of a Pioneer Men's Group*, Element Books, Rockport, MA. 1996.

- Masters, Robert Augustus, *To Be a Man: A Guide to True Masculine Power*, Sounds True, Boulder, CO, 2015.

- Miller, Stuart, *Men and Friendship*. Gateway Books, London, 1983.

- Moore, Robert and Gillette, Doug, *King, Warrior, Magician, Lover: Rediscovering the Archetypes of the Mature Masculine*, HarperCollins, San Francisco, 1990.

- Moore, Robert, and Gillette, Doug, *The King Within: Accessing the King in the Male Psyche*, William Morrow and Company, New York, 1992.

- Moore, Robert, and Gillette, Doug, *The Warrior Within: Accessing the Knight in the Male Psyche*, William Morrow and Company, New York, 1992.

- Osherson, Samuel, *Wrestling with Love: How Men Struggle with Intimacy*, Fawcett Columbine, New York, 1992.

- Sexton, Jared, *The Man They Wanted Me to Be: Toxic Masculinity and a Crisis of Our Own Making*, Counterpoint, Berkeley, CA, 2019.

- Stein, Joel, *Man Made: A Stupid Quest for Masculinity*, Grand Central Publishing, New York, 2012.

- Wineland, John, *From the Core: A New Masculine Paradigm for Leading with Love, Living Your Truth, and Healing the World*, Sounds True Publisher, Boulder, CO, 2022.

MULTICULTURAL AWARENESS

- Adams, Maurianne and Bell, Lee Ann, *Teaching for Diversity and Social Justice, 3rd Edition*, Routledge Publisher, New York, 2016.

- Jacobs, Bruce A., *Race Manners for the 21st Century*, Arcade Publishing, New York, 2006.

- Kivel, Paul, *Uprooting Racism: How White People Can Work for Racial Justice*, New Society Publishers, Canada, 2002.

- Kimmel, Michael, *The Gendered Society*, Oxford University Press, New York, 2000.

- Kimmel, Michael, *Angry White Men: American Masculinity at the End of an Era*, Nation books, New York, 2013.

- Ukockis, Gail, *Misogyny: The New Activism*, Oxford University Press, New York, 2019.

RAISING BOYS

- Baldoni, Justin, *Boys Will Be Human: A Get-Real Gut-Check Guide to Becoming the Strongest, Kindest, Bravest Person You Can Be*, Harper, New York, 2022.

- Gouveia, Aaron, *Raising Boys to Be Good Men: A Parent's Guide to Bringing Up Happy Sons in a World Filled with Toxic Masculinity*, Skyhorse Publishing, New York, 2020.

- Gurian, Michael, *The Wonder of Boys*, Tarcher/Putnam, New York, 1997.

- Nerburn, Kent, *Letters to My Son: A Father's Wisdom on Manhood, Women, Life and Love*, Novato, CA, 1994.

- Pollack, William, *Real Boys: Rescuing Our Sons from the Myths of Boyhood*, Random House, New York, 1998.

- Silverstein, Olga, and Rashbaum, Beth, *The Courage to Raise Good Men*, Viking Press, New York, 1994.

- Thomas, T, *Men Surviving Incest: A Male Survivor Shares on the Process of Recovery*, Launch Press, San Francisco, 1989.

RELATIONSHIPS

- Albere, Patricia, *Evolutionary Relationships: Unleashing the Power of Mutual Awakening*, Oracle Institute Pres, Independence, VA, 2017.

- Baer, Greg, *Real Love: The Truth about Unconditional Love and Fulfilling Relationships*, Gotham Books, New York, 2003.

- Chapman, Gary, *The Five Love Languages: The Secret to Love That Lasts*, Northfield Publishing, Chicago, IL, 2015.

- Frank, Mari, and Szymczak, Leonard, *Fighting for Love: Turn Conflict into Intimacy*, Porpoise Press, Laguna Nigel, CA, 2016.

- Gerek, Destin, *The Evolved Masculine: Be the Man the World Needs & The One She Craves*, Archetypal Publishing, 2019.

- Gray, John, *Men Are from Mars, Women Are from Venus*. Harper Collins, New York, 1992.

- Hendrix, Harville, *Getting the Love You Want: A Guide for Couples*, Owl Books, New York, 1988.

- Levant, Ronald, with Kopecky, Gini, *Masculinity Reconstructed: Changing the Rules of Manhood—at Work, in Relationships and in Family Life*. Penguin, New York, 1996.

- Real, Terry, *How Can I Get Through to You? Reconnecting Men and Women*, Scribner, New York, 2002.

- Real, Terry, *The New Rules of Marriage: What You Need to Know to Make Love Work*, Ballantine Books, New York, 2007.

- Real, Terry, *Us: Getting Past You and Me to Build a More Loving Relationship*, Goop Press/Rodale, New York, 2022.

- Tannen, Deborah, *You Just Don't Understand: Women and Men in Conversation*. Ballantine, New York, 1990.

SEXUALITY

- Anand, Margo, *The Art of Sexual Ecstasy: The Path of Sacred Sexuality for Western Lovers*, Jeremy Tarcher, Los Angeles, 1989.

- Bearman, Steve, "Why Are Men So Obsessed with Sex?,?" *Elephant Journal*, October 13, 2013.

- Deida, David, *Finding God Through Sex: A Spiritual Guide to Ecstatic Loving and Deep Passion for Men and Women*, Plexus, 2002.

- Deida, David, *Intimate Communion: Awakening Your Sexual Essence*, Health Communications, Inc., Deerfield Beach, FL, 1995.

- Diamond, Jed, *The Warrior's Journey Home: Healing Men, Healing the Planet*, New Harbinger Publications, Oakland, CA, 1994.

- Goldman, Ronald, *Circumcision, The Hidden Trauma: How an American Cultural Practice Affects Infants and Ultimately Us All*, Vanguard Publications, New York, 1997.

- Jordan, Judith, et. al., *Women's Growth in Connection: Writings from the Stone Center*, Guilford Press, New York, 1991.

- Moore, Thomas, *The Soul of Sex: Cultivating Life as an Act of Love*, Harper Collins, New York, 1998.

- Perel, Esther, *Mating in Captivity: Unlocking Erotic Intelligence*, Harper, New York, 2007.

- Richardson, Dana, and Richardson, Michael, *Tantric Sex for Men: Making Love a Meditation*, Destiny Books, Rochester, VT, 2010

- Schnarch, Dr. David, *Passionate Marriage: Love, Sex and Intimacy in Emotionally Committed Relationships*, W.W. Norton and Co., New York, 1997.

SPIRITUALITY

- Broniec, Rick, *The Seven Generations Story: An Incentive to Change Yourself, Your Family and the Planet*, Crescendo Publishing, Carlsbad, CA, 2015.

- Jackson, Phil, and Delehanty, Hugh, *Sacred Hoops: Spiritual Lessons of a Hardwood Warrior*, Hyperion, New York, 1995.

- Rohr, Richard, *From Wild Man to Wise Man: Reflections on Male Spirituality*, Franciscan Media, Cincinnati, OH, 2005.

- Szymczak, Leonard, *The Roadmap Home: Your GPS To Inner Peace*, BookSurge Publishing, North Charleston, SC, 2009.

- Thornton, James, *A Field Guide to the Soul: A down-to-Earth Handbook of Spiritual Practice*, Bell Tower, New York, 2000.

- Tolle, Eckart, *A New Earth: Awakening to Your Life's Purpose*, Penguin Group, New York, 2005.

- Williamson, Marianne, *A Return to Love*, Foundation for Inner Peace, Harper Collins, New York, 1992.

- Yiamouyiannis, Zeus, *The Spiritually Confident Man: Pioneering a New Frontier of Co-creative Masculinity*, Phoenix Transformation Media, Phoenix, 2018.

Acknowledgements

It takes a community to publish a book. Therefore, we want to recognize and offer our thanks to the following people.

Robert Bly, author of *Iron John*, is often considered the grandfather of the men's movement that started to flourish in the 70s into the 90s. Even though Robert recently passed, we want to acknowledge him and the other visionaries who wrote books and ran workshops to move us to a place where we learned new ways of being men and brothers. Many of these leaders have touched our lives personally in workshops and conferences. It would take paragraphs to recognize them all, but we want to highlight a few: Robert Moore, Michael Meade, James Hillman, Bill Kauth, Ron Hering, Rich Tosi,

Douglas Gillette, Warren Farrell, Aaron Kipnis, Sam Keen, John Lee, Buddy Portugal, and Bob Mark.

We also want to thank Mark Greene for his insightful foreword, Mary Harris and Glenda Rynn for their excellent feedback and editing, Pam Sheppard for her insightful book consultations, Fiona Jayde for the amazing cover, and Tamara Cribley for designing the interior of the book.

We wish to acknowledge those in our Beta readers group. They provided wonderful feedback and encouragement, chapter by chapter, to help us climb the publishing mountain: Harry Tucker, Linda Savage, Michele Lyons, Carl Foster, Glenda Rynn, Mari Frank, Bill Motlong, Arthur Tassinello, and David Gruder.

Others who have helped include Catherine Clinch, Mike Hernacki, David Heiman, Jerry Fleck, Steve Pumphrey, Vladi,

Brandon Hall, Jim Lee, Danna Beal, Peter Gray, Larry Porricelli, Sharon Goldinger, Daniel Midson-Short, John Barry, Kay Knight, Michelle Strbich, and Dane Wright.

We value the following groups that have supported this book: ManKind Project, Southern California Writers Association, North County Circle, Victories for Men, and Toastmasters. Finally, to our family and friends for their encouragement and support.

Thank you all!

About the Authors

Leonard Szymczak, MSW, LCSW is a writer, international speaker, psychotherapist, and life coach. For the past 40 years, he has worked in both Australia and America as an educator, writer, and therapist. He was a director of a Family Therapy Program in Sydney, Australia, and later worked with the Family Institute at Northwestern University. He has had a wide range of clinical services with men including a crisis intervention program with a police department, treatment of adolescent males, and men's therapy groups. As a result, he has been in the forefront of men's healing for 40 years.

He is an award-winning author. His books include *The Roadmap Home: Your GPS to Inner Peace*, an Amazon bestseller, as well as four novels. He is the co-author, along with Mari Frank, of *Fighting for Love: Turn Conflict into Intimacy*.

Leonard's TEDx talk on fatherhood has been viewed over 110,000 times. He is an international speaker and workshop presenter and maintains a counseling and coaching practice in Orange County, CA. Leonard is the proud father of two adult children and four grandchildren.

For more information about Leonard, contact him at:
leonard@leonardsz.com
www.leonardsz.com
www.FightingForLoveNow.com
www.facebook.com/leonardszymczakauthor

Rick Broniec, M.Ed. is an author, inspirational speaker, coach, and workshop facilitator. He has been a sought after leader of men's trainings internationally since 1987. He has facilitated hundreds of men's personal growth and leadership workshops on five continents and eleven countries for thousands of men which gives him a unique window into the needs of modern men. Rick is also passionately involved in multicultural awareness work. Having spoken extensively around the world, he co-created several multicultural trainings, including *Unpacking Power, Privilege, and Difference* and *Power, Privilege and Difference in the Workplace.*

Rick is an Amazon bestseller author of *The Seven Generations Story: An Incentive to Heal Yourself, Your Family and the Planet* and *A Passionate Life: 7 Steps for Reclaiming Your Passion, Purpose and Joy.* Rick has been anthologized in *1 Habit: 100 Habits from the Happiest Achievers on the Planet.*

Besides being in partnership in his business, Wisdom Windfall, LLC, Rick consults for the international, not-for-profit men's healing organization called the ManKind Project. Rick continues to actively lead and train men around the world.

Rick is proud of his three daughters and crazy in love with his four granddaughters. He loves riding his Harley Davidson motorcycle.

For more information about Rick, contact him at:
rbroniec@gmail.com
www.PowerToolsForMen.org
www.WisdomWindfall.com

Note from the Authors

Thanks for reading *Power Tools for Men*. If you enjoyed this book, please consider leaving a review online at your favorite store's website.

May we all work together to build a better future!
Leonard Szymczak & Rick Broniec

For more information on this book, contact:
powertoolsformen@gmail.com
www.PowerToolsForMen.org
www.facebook.com/toolstohelpmenthrive

Made in United States
Cleveland, OH
03 December 2024

11310653R00148